Top School ESSAYS

Published by :
Lotus Press Publishers & Distributors

Top School ESSAYS

Sneha Yadav

Lotus PRESS

4735/22, Prakash Deep Building
Ansari Road, Darya Ganj,
New Delhi - 110002

Lotus Press : Publishers & Distributors
Unit No. 220, 2nd Floor, 4735/22, Prakash Deep Building,
Ansari Road, Darya Ganj, New Delhi- 110002
Ph.: 41325510,98118-38000
• E-mail : lotuspress1984@gmail.com
www.lotuspress.co.in

Top School Essays

ISBN: 978-81-8382-222-0

Printed & Published by : **Lotus Press Publisher & Distributors,** New Delhi-02

CONTENTS

Chapter 1

What is an Essay

In simple terms, sentences are collections of words. Paragraphs are collections of sentences. Finally, essays are collections of paragraphs.

An essay is usually a short piece of writing that is often written from an author's point of view, expressing his views and observations.

It is a non-fiction piece of writing that has a definable beginning, middle and an ending.

Each essay is built around a central idea. This theme is the glue that binds the essay together. It's what the essay is about, what it intends to show, prove, or do in more than two paragraphs. Though two and one paragraph essays are also possible, yet they don't appear so in the strictest form.

At the same time, length of a paragraph or an essay is not a primary consideration when writing an essay. It should be able to put forward the main concept in the best possible manner. The primary job of an essay is to discuss its main concept or central theme.

Types of Essay

There are different types of essays and each warrants a different style of writing. Therefore, the first thing to do is to focus on reason for writing the essay.

Although the basic essay outline will remain the same irrespective of the tone of the essay, one can work towards making a powerful impact by deciding the tone and mood of the essay beforehand.

An index of essays for you to choose from would include argumentative essays, descriptive essays, narrative essays and persuasive essays. Each one of these requires its own kind of writing.

Narrative Essay

Narrative essays tell stories. So, putting together a good narrative essay would require more simple wordings. For such essays, one must employ their expressive powers well enough to be able to paint a clear picture for the readers so that they can actually see - rather than read about - a scene or a character in their own mind's eye.

You do not have to worry about how to write a narrative essay. It is just like telling someone a story, but here the challenge is to be able to draw the person into your story and to get the readers to feel for the central characters.

A sample narrative essay topic is a topic like "My Trip to Historical Monument". The key to writing a good narrative essay is to write on a topic that is close to your heart. This way you just have to translate your own emotions into the words you pen down.

While narrating your story, you must be able to make your point or the central theme of the essay clear to the reader.

In all narrative essays, the concluding paragraph has tremendous significance. This is where the writer must re-affirm his or her viewpoint in such a manner as to render a powerful impact on the reader.

Descriptive Essay

One of the most challenging forms of essay writing is writing descriptive essays. The best descriptive essays are those in which the writer knows and understands the subjects extremely well. The writer must then find the right words to project his or her views and imagery onto the readers of his or her work. The writer's choice of words has major importance because it would change the way, the reader visualises or feels for the central object of the essay.

One can draw comparisons between objects to highlight the difference between the central object in the essay and others. A good and easy way to learn about different descriptive writing techniques is to read through such essays.

Students today have right of entry to many free descriptive essay resources and it would be worthwhile to go through example descriptive essay pieces available through various sources.

As with all types of essay writing, the writer's choice of subject makes a big difference. For instance, if you choose to write about a place or event that really affected you emotionally, you will find it that much easier to describe.

Persuasive Essay

Persuasive essay writing is all about being able to get the reader to see your viewpoint and to guide the reader to your way of thinking. Hence, it is advisable to choose ideas for persuasive essay topics on the basis of what subjects move you the most.

Since these essays require your motivation to be your driving force, you should make sure that you choose an essay that supports your own opinions on an issue.

While choosing persuasive essay topics, one must remember that the writers need to use their sense of reasoning effectively enough to convince the reader that their viewpoint is the correct one. Issues like diet, fashion, tradition, culture etc. can make excellent subjects for persuasive essays.

The goal of the persuasive essay-writer is to appeal to the reader's sense of right and wrong in such a way as to convince the reader to ditch his or her own ideas.

This can only be achieved by presenting the reader with accurate facts and figures. Hence, researching the material is absolutely essential in the case of persuasive essays.

Argumentative Essay

Argumentative essays present one side of an argument. The goal here is to be as convincing as possible so that the reader is influenced into adopting your line of thought. For writing argumentative essays effectively, one must first be sure of his or her own point-of-view on a subject. It can be really difficult to write an essay advocating a viewpoint that is not truly what you believe. Hence, it is advisable to pick a subject to write on that is not opposing to your own views and beliefs.

Equipping yourself with sufficient facts and figures is part of the job though. It is just as important to present the information you collect in such a way that it manages to impress and convince rather than bore the reader.

Argumentative essay topics can range from anything like it could be some major political issue to topics like The Role of Women in Modern-day Indian Society. Some examples of argumentative essays are, Global Warming, The Need for School Uniforms, etc.

It is absolutely imperative to workout an argumentative essay outline right at the start of such a project. This helps one organise his or her thoughts. This is really important because without an outline to guide you through, you run the risk of writing too much on one point and therefore neglecting to mention or inadequately expressing the others.

How to Write Essays

Essay writing is an art of displaying information on a piece of paper that is intended to take a position in favour or against an issue. It can also be use as a tool to gather mass attention over a single point.

Writing essays is a task that requires talent as well as technique of presentation and creating interest for readers to engage till the end. It doesn't mean that only select group of people with God gifted talent can write essay, but it is a difficult job to do; that's for sure. Here are some tips that can help you in writing essays as well as in avoiding common mistakes that beginners usually do:

1. **Plan you writing process:** Start with choosing an essay topic that you like most or are very strong over it. Now, focus on your ideas on what you want reader to understand. Set an outline and stick to it till the end.

   Your outline ideally should include introduction, your view statement and conclusion, proofread and edit as per requirement.

2. **Stay on purpose:** Make sure that your essay meets all the requirements - it is focused on a single issue and is easy to read and understand for general readers. Don't just provide

information, rather give your arguments and try to illustrate your point in a defined manner.

3. **Don't forget the basics:** It is important that you don't forget the basics of essay writing, such as managing your time by not involving in complex statements, answering the question clearly, and above all not providing copied material. Remember, people don't want to waste time on things that they can easily find on internet, you need to come up with original thoughts to maintain reader's interest.

Talking about essay writing tips, you need to avoid some common mistakes also, such as the following:

1. **Don't put useless items:** It sounds good to fill it up with loads of information to give away a decent impression of your knowledge and ability as a writer, but the reality is that people will just waste seconds to scroll down to decide whether they can digest all this useless item or not!
2. **Don't copy other's ideas:** That's another famous policy of beginners who seems to lack confidence on their own skills and search for cool ideas on internet and other sources. Today's readers are smart enough to pick the tone of essay. Copying will not just reduce the readership, but it will hurt the reputation of the writer badly.
3. **Choosing an easy topic:** If it's easy for you to understand, then it's same for other people also. Always choose a topic that people wants to read about, but is not well supplied by writers.

Sentence Writing Tips

In essay writing sentence structure and flow is very important. These two things are very important to writing as they greatly affect readers.

You are about to read some of the most valuable essay writing tips on which English teachers mostly stress because they are central for developing good writing skills. Applying these strategies to your writing will greatly improve your clarity in essay writing. Furthermore, once you consciously get into the habit of using them regularly, you would find that your good writing skills would aid you in any career field.

Transition between Sentences and Paragraphs

Writing is just like having an actual conversation except for the fact that readers cannot ask you a question if they don't understand something you just said. With that being said, having intermediary phrases and sentences in between your ideas would greatly help your ideas to flow.

Transitions are also a great way to show similar or opposite ideas in your writing. For instance, phrases or words such as: in addition, furthermore, also, and additionally tell your reader that you are adding related ideas to your previous sentence.

On the other hand, words phrases like: conversely, alternatively, then again, on the other hand, and in contrast, the tell reader that you are discussing an idea that opposes your previous sentence's idea.

While finding changeover words between sentences can be accessed by the use of thesaurus, transitioning between paragraphs gets a little tougher.

With paragraphs, it is necessary to have previous paragraph flow into the next one by introducing the next paragraph's idea in the last sentence of previous paragraph. After that, the first sentence of next paragraph will now talk about the new idea in it.

Sentence Variety

Sentence variety refers to the length of sentences. If one writes short sentences one after another, his or her writing will seem variable. On the other hand, if one writes long sentences one after another, reader might get lost in ideas. In both instances, readers will lose interest in whatever you're discussing because they cannot follow your train of thought.

Sentence variety is one of the easiest essay writing tips to adapt because it allows you to make your essay exciting by simply varying the length of your sentences. Let's take the first paragraph of this section (sentence variety) as an example. You will notice that the first two sentences are short and direct while the last two sentences are longer and more elaborate. This strategy becomes easier to incorporate into writing skills because even though you may not have sentence variety in your first draft, you can go back and make the necessary changes.

Passive *vs.* Active Voice

Passive voice is the sign of wordiness. The passive voice is usually in the form of 'to be' (is, are, was, were, be, been) followed by the past participle (*hint*: looks like a past tense verb).

For example:

Passive voice: The neighborhood fire was started by a lightning strike.

Active voice: The lightning strike started the neighbourhood fire.

Do you see the difference? The sentence in the active voice is much more direct and clear.

Stick to Your Thesis

A thesis is created for a reason and that is to argue writer's point of view regarding a particular topic. The whole essay should support writer's argument with many little arguments and evidences.

The writer should write his thesis in a small piece of paper. Then, he should place this piece of paper right next to each of his paragraphs. After that, he should read each paragraph and compare it to his thesis. This process allowed him to catch any paragraphs in his essay that are 'off topic' and revised them accordingly.

Reliable References and Records

This is probably one of the most common essay writing tips. To avoid using untrustworthy resources, writer should always look into peer reviewed articles in research papers or articles that are published in a well-known newspaper. These publications make an extra effort to providing good, reliable information because they have a name to conserve.

Timc

If there was one thing that students can do to improve their writing, it would be to give themselves enough time to write. Many students tend to delay about their writing assignments that they do not have time to edit or review their work before they turn it in. Besides having the chance to review and edit your essay, you can get the chance to take a break from it for a day or two so that you can look at it in a whole new light when you read it again.

Peer-review

If you wrote a 5-page essay and felt that you really did a good job, you probably would not edit it further. On the other hand, if your classmates or friends read it, they may be able to find spelling mistakes, grammatical errors or arguments that can be better supported. Thus, having your essay reviewed by somebody else who would give you that one extra chance to get their opinion before you present your essay before the target readers.

The Word 'it'

Often, it is not good to use 'it' at the beginning of any sentence. Just replacing the word it with the actual word, makes your writing much more clear to your reader and this avoids confusion.

Essay writing tips would not help you become a better writer unless you practice them regularly. So practice writing and become good writer.

CHAPTER 2

Sample Essays

Computer – The Human's Greatest Invention

Man has made several inventions. Computer is one of them. The computer has begun to control so many critical functions that today man is excessively proud about his invention. Today, the computer plays an important role in our lives and we are completely dependent on him.

It has been commonly said that the computer can never replace the human brain, as it is created by humans, but we can't ignore the fact that computer is much more capable than human brain. There are many ways in which the computer has an edge over man. The computer has the capability to evaluate problems that man can hardly imagine.

Even if a man can calculate the same problems as a computer, the computer can do it faster with 100% accuracy. The computer is clearly superior in many other aspects. In absolute speed of computation and retrieval of data, the computer is obviously by far the stronger. It has the capacity to handle things on a far bigger scale than the human brain could ever do. Measurements, results, applications can all be done to the smallest details, far beyond the human brain's capabilities.

Calculations can be done with accuracy nearly impossible. The human brain is easily stressed out by events and loses effectiveness when tired but computer can't.

On the other hand, though the human brain has a lot of flaws, yet it also has an edge over the computer. It has the capacity to create, unlike the computer and it can work without full input, making logical assumptions about problems.

A person can work with a wide variety of methods, seeing new, more efficient ways of handling problems. It can come up with infinite ways of getting around problems encountered in day to day life, while a computer has a limited memory of new tricks it can come up with, limited by its programming.

It is the human brain that figures out the programming that will allow any improvements for the computer. The human brain can learn to understand anything. It can grasp the central concept of anything.

Also, emotions are not capable in a computer. Emotions and feeling allow the human brain to evolve beyond a problem-solving machine. They open the mind to an endless realm of possibilities. The reason why computers cannot create is because of the lack of emotions.

In conclusion, computers have become the necessity of modern life, yet they are far from perfection. They have only a limited capacity for learning. The computer lacks the common sense of the human brain. On the human brain has many flaws, just as it has advantages. The human brain can never perform tasks as efficiently or as tirelessly as the computer.

Emotions make the mind dangerously unstable; A man's performance is subject to moods and emotional disruption. The computer suffers no such problems.

Emotions blur the human brain's capacity to make clear, logical decisions. We can say that the computer is the best invention of man, but only when it is operated with human brain.

■■■

Friendship

Friendship is a relationship that has many dimensions and styles. Friendship can be between any two or more persons and there is no compulsion of age, gender, geography, race, creed or nationality. People living in a house or living anywhere in this world are equally to prone to the relationship of friendship. Friendship has no boundaries and no limits.

In life every one will meet many people who say that they are your friends, but you will make only a few true friends. What is a friend? In the dictionary, a friend is defined as one that is not hostile, or one attached to another by affection or esteem, a favoured companion. In my opinion, a friend is much more than that. A friend is someone that will stand by you, even during the toughest times. Friendship is about believing in your friends and helping them to achieve all they can or want to do in life. We are there for each other with hugs, advice, kind words, fights, and anger, whatever comes along. When the day ends, we are still friends who have each other no matter what happens.

We all have a desire to have friends. It is what makes us reach out of our shells and take the chance of being hurt. It is not easy figuring out who is a friend and who is not. I believe Divya, to be a true friend. We met in school and have known each other for five years. Divya and I have been through many good and hard times together. In addition, we have experienced so many together, such as travelling to Goa and the South India where we shared many enjoyable moments. Our friendship has done nothing but has grown over the years and continues to do so. We are currently indulgencing in another adventure by living together in Pune.

I consider Divya to be a true friend. A true friend is there for you when you need them. To have a true friend is a remarkable thing. To find someone who shares similar interests, who cares about whom you are and what you are doing... true friend is there for you when you need them. He or she is someone who you are not embarrassed to cry in front of, to whom you can tell the deepest, darkest secrets, knowing they will be safe. An old rule of thumb is that a true friend is someone you can call after months or even years and speak as if not a day had passed. Divya and I have experienced this, we were parted from each other for about a year and half while she was away at her exams and I had moved back to my home in Delhi to spend some time with my mom. Once we came in contact again with each other to attend university it was as though we never skipped a beat.

True friendships come along rarely, and so I am thankful to have met her that we must move past anything that threatens our friendship and see the big picture. Without our friendships, we are indeed lost. Whatever happens, we should always keep our true friends close to our heart. Tell your friends how much they mean to you. Do not let them slip away. If they do, go out and get them back. The bonds we make during these days will serve to keep us going in the months and years ahead.

■■■

ELECTIONS - Foundation of Democracy

Elections form the foundation of democracy. They are the central institution of democratic representative governments. It is not only legal, but also a moral responsibility of a democratic nation to hold free and fair elections. It is true that all modern democracies hold elections.

But at the same time, it is also true that all elections are not democratic. Right-wing dictatorships, communalist, and single-party governments also stage elections to make their rule. Such parties represent only one candidate or a list of candidates. Such circumstances allow no alternative choices to the voter.

Though such elections may offer several candidates for each area, it is usually ensured through pressure or supports that only the government approved candidate is chosen. Other elections may offer genuine choices- but only within the serving party. These are not democratic elections.

Democratic Elections

"Democratic elections are competitive, periodic, comprehensive, definitive elections in which the chief decision-makers in a government are selected by citizens who enjoy broad freedom to criticise government, to publish their criticism and to present alternatives," says Jeane Kirkpatrick, scholar and former U.S. ambassador to the United Nations.

Democratic elections are competitive. The opposition, whether it consists of one party or many as well as all the candidates in an election must enjoy the freedom of speech, assembly, and movement necessary to speak their mind. A true democracy allows criticism of the government. Democracy also allows all the parties to bring alternative policies and candidates to the voters. Simply permitting all access to the ballot is not enough in a true democracy. A democracy in which all the parties are not allowed a fair use of media to generate awareness in the public règarding their view, agenda etc. certainly cannot be called a democracy.

Moreover a country where the campaigning rallies of the candidates or the parties other than the ruling one are harassed or where newspapers indulge in yellow journalism victimising a particular candidate or a party also cannot be called democratic. The party in power may enjoy the advantages of incumbency, but the rules and conduct of the election contest must be fair.

Democratic elections are periodic. A democracy like India holds elections after a specific period of time. In India, polling time is after every five years. Democracies do not elect dictators or presidents-for-life.

Even a successfully running government is required to seek the approval of the common man after its term is over. Moreover, the elected officials are answerable to the people, as it is the same people whose votes hold the power to elect them again or choose a new government.

Thus, it is quite obvious that the elected government cannot go on fooling the people with empty promises. The promises made to the common man are to be fulfilled else the power would slip out of the hands of the government resulting into a new government.

Democratic elections are comprehensive. The definition of citizen and voter must be large enough to include a large proportion of the adult population. A government chosen by a small, exclusive group is not a democracy. Thus, all the members of the minorities irrespective of racial, tribal, or religious factors or gender issues should be allowed full citizenship with the right to vote.

Democratic elections are definitive. They determine the leadership of the government. The elected representatives rule subject to the laws and constitution of the country.

Democracies flourish in the act of voting itself. To cast a pressure free ballot, voters in a democracy must be permitted to cast their ballots in secret.

Thus, the votes are confidential. At the same time, the protection of the ballot box and tallying of vote totals must be conducted as openly as possible, so that citizens are confident that the results are accurate.

■■■

Indian Cinema

In India, cinema is very near to the lives of people or we can say that it is in the heart of the people. The large screen provides an alternative, an escape from the realities of day-to-day life. People cry, laugh, sing, dance and enjoy emotions through cinema.

The study of Indian cinema would throw light on the progress of technology, especially cinematography, and the changing political scene and social values and attitudes. The first films were the silent films launched by Phalke, which had titles in English, Gujarati, Hindi and Urdu, related to myths and legends. The stories were familiar to the audience and required minimum commentary. Historical also proved very popular; Harsh, Chandragupta, Ashoka and the Mughal and Maratha kings won the silver screen.

While Phalke was the father of Indian cinema, Irani was the father of the talkie. He produced his first talkie, Alam Ara, in 1931. The classic Hollywood musical 'Singing in the Rain' exemplifies the cynicism with which people first regarded the talking movie and this holds good for India too.

If Bombay (Now Mumbai) was the hub of early cinema, the other centres were not far behind-Calcutta (Now Kolkata) and Madras (Now Chennai) were also making path-breaking films in the initial years of Indian Cinema. Like cinema in Bengal, Malayalam, Tamil, Kanad cinema too was meaningful, but it took a longer time to get noticed. The seventies saw an unhealthy divide between the existing commercial or mainstream cinema and the new parallel cinema or art films.

Fortunately, this situation did not last long, for soon there came a crop of filmmakers who realised that meaningful films need not incur heavy losses. It was only after the government set up the Film Finance Corporation (FFC, which in 1980 came to be known as NFDC i.e. National Film Development Corporation) that several small but serious filmmakers got the wherewithal to make films. The eighties saw the passion of women filmmakers, Vijaya Mehta (Rao Saheb), Aparna Sen (36, Chowringhee Lane, Paroma), Sai Paranjpye (Chashme Baddoor, Katha, Sparsh), Kalpana Laxmi (Ek Pal and, later the much acclaimed Rudali), Prema Karanth (Phaniamma) and Meera Nair (Salaam Bombay). The most commendable thing about these directors is their individuality. Their films have strong content and are told with passion.

In the nineties, Indian cinema faced tough competition from television; the cable network gave viewers number of channels and due to this the cinema halls took a beating. Nevertheless, films like Aditya Chopra's maiden effort 'Dilwale Dulhaniya Le Jayenge' and Suraj Barjatya's 'Hum Aapke Hain Kaun' broke all records, because they recalled the innocence of the fifties, a novelty in this age of sex and violence. This gave hope. In 2000, the movies were more based on technologies and effects. Rakesh Roshan's 'Koi Mil Gaya' and 'Krish' broke all records. These stories are based on aliens and made by advanced technologies. Similarly, 'Dhoom-1' and 'Dhoom-2' are technology and thrill based movies.

In India, cinema can never die. It has gone too deep into our mind. It may undergo several changes in future. With other mediums opening up, there will be a smaller market for films. We are living in a global world and we are becoming a judicious audience. No one can fool us, only the best will survive and this is just as well.

Global Warming

Global warming is an increase in the average temperature of the earth's temperature, especially a sustained change sufficient to cause climate change. The average facade temperature of the globe has increased more than 1 degree since 1900 and the speed of warming has been almost three folds the century long average since 1970. This increase in earth's average temperature is called Global warming. More or less all specialists studying the climate record of the earth have the same opinion now that human actions, mainly the discharge of green house gases from smokestacks, vehicles, and burning forests, are perhaps the leading power driving the fashion. The gases append to the planet's normal greenhouse effect, permitting sunlight in, but stopping some of the ensuing heat from burning back to space. Based on the study on past climate shifts, notes of current situations, and computer simulations, many climate scientists say that lacking of big curbs in greenhouse gas discharges, the 21st century might see temperatures rise of about 3 to 8 degrees, climate patterns piercingly shift, ice sheets contract and seas rise several feet. With the probable exemption of one more world war, a huge asteroid, a fatal plague, or global warming may be the only worst dangers to our planet earth.

Global Warming Causes

The major cause of global warming is the release of green house gases like carbon dioxide, methane, nitrous oxide etc. into the atmosphere. The major source of carbon dioxide is the power plants. These power plants emit large amounts of carbon dioxide produced from burning of fossil fuels for the purpose of electricity generation. About twenty percent of carbon dioxide emitted in the atmosphere comes from burning of gasoline in the engines of the vehicles. Buildings, both commercial and residential represent a larger source of global warming pollution than cars and trucks.

Building of these structures require a lot of fuel to be burnt which emits a large amount of carbon dioxide in the atmosphere. Methane is more than 20 times as effectual as CO_2 at entrapping heat in the atmosphere. Methane is obtained from resources such as rice paddies, bovine flatulence, bacteria in bogs and fossil fuel manufacture. The main sources of nitrous oxide include nylon and nitric acid production, cars with catalytic converters, and the use of fertilisers in agriculture and the burning of organic matter. Another cause of global warming is deforestation that is caused by cutting and burning of forests for the purpose of residence and industrialisation.

Scientists all over the world are making predictions about the ill effects of Global warming and connecting some of the events that have taken place in the past few decades as an alarm of global warming. The effect of global warming is increasing the average temperature of the earth. A rise in earth's temperatures can in turn cause to other alterations in the ecology, including an increasing sea level and modifying the quantity and pattern of rainfall. These modifications may boost the occurrence and concentration of severe climate events, such as floods, famines, heat waves, tornados, and twisters. Other consequences may comprise of higher or lower agricultural outputs, glacier melting, lesser summer stream flows, genus extinctions and rise in the ranges of disease vectors. As an effect of global warming, many species of birds and animals have already become extinct. As an effect of global warming various new diseases have emerged lately. It is expected that many species will die off or become extinct due to the increase in the temperatures of the water, whereas various other species, which prefer warmer waters, will increase tremendously. Perhaps the most disturbing changes are expected in the coral reefs that are expected to die off as an effect of global warming. The global warming is expected to cause irreversible changes in the ecosystem and the behaviour of animals. Birds are a species that will be affected by a change in the climate. Global warming might result in birds finding a more permanent home in northern areas in the Northern Hemisphere.

The scientists tell us that the tundra is in danger of melting due to an amount of extra global warming pollution that is equivalent to the net amount that is previously in the earth's atmosphere. Likewise, earlier one more team of scientists reported that in a single year Greenland witnessed 32 glacial earthquakes between 4.6 and 5.1 on the Richter scale. This is a disturbing sign and points that a huge destabilisation that may now be in progress deep within the second biggest growth of ice on the planet. This ice would be enough to raise sea level 20 feet worldwide if it broke up and slipped into the sea. Each day passing brings yet new proof that we are now in front of a global emergency, a climate emergency that needs instant action to shrilly decrease carbon dioxide emissions worldwide in order to turn down the earth's rising temperatures and avoid any calamity.

It is not easy to attach any particular event to global warming, but studies prove the fact that human activities are increasing the earth's temperature. Even though most predictions focus on the epoch up to 2100, even if no further greenhouse gases were discharged after this date, global warming and sea level would be likely to go on to rise for more than a millennium, since carbon dioxide has a long average atmospheric life span.

Many efforts are being made by various nations to cut down the rate of global warming. One such effort is the Kyoto agreement that has been made between various nations to reduce the emissions of various green house gases. Also, many non profit organisations are working for the cause. Al Gore was one of the foremost U.S. politicians to heave an alarm about the hazards of global warming. He has produced a significantly acclaimed documentary movie called "*An Inconvenient Truth*," and has written a book that archives his advice that Earth is dashing toward an immensely warmer future. Al Gore, has given various speeches to raise an awareness of global warming. He has warned people about the ill effects of Global warming and its remedies.

The future of emissions damage depends on several factors, demographics, economics, technology, policies and institutional developments. Future predictions do not look good for this planet if nothing is done soon.

■■■

Father of the Nation

Mohandas Karamchand Gandhi was a great freedom fighter. He was born in the town of Porbander in Gujarat on 2 October 1869. He had done his schooling in nearby Rajkot. At that time, India was under British. His father died before Gandhi could finish his schooling. At the young age of thirteen, he was married to Kasturba who was even younger. In 1888, Gandhi set sail for England, where he had decided to pursue a degree in law.

After one year of a none too successful law practice, Gandhi decided to accept an offer from an Indian businessman in South Africa, Dada Abdulla, to join him as a legal adviser. The Indians who had been living in South Africa were without political rights, and were generally known by the derogatory name of 'coolies'.

Gandhi himself came to an awareness of the frightening force when he thrown out of a first-class railway compartment car, though he held a first-class ticket, at Pietermaritzburg. From this political awakening, Gandhi was to emerge as the leader of the Indian community, and it was in South Africa that he first coined the term *satyagraha* to signify his theory and practice of non-violent resistance.

Gandhi described himself as a seeker of *satya* (truth), which could not be attained other than through *ahinsa* (non-violence, love) and *brahmacharya* (celibacy, striving towards God).

Gandhi returned to India in early 1915, and never left the country. Over the next few years, he was to become involved in numerous local struggles, such as at Champaran in Bihar, where workers on indigo plantations complained of oppressive working conditions, and at Ahmedabad, where a dispute had broken out between management and workers at textile mills.

Gandhi had ideas on every subject, from hygiene and nutrition to education and labor, and he relentlessly pursued his ideas in newspaper. He would still be remembered as one of the principal figures in the history of Indian journalism.

By this time he had earned the title of *Mahatma* from Rabindranath Tagore, India's most well-known writer. When tragedy happened in the Jallianwala Bagh in Amritsar Gandhi wrote the report of the Punjab Congress Inquiry Committee.

Over the next two years, Gandhi initiated the non-cooperation movement, which called upon Indians to withdraw from British institutions, to return honours conferred by the British, and to learn the art of self-reliance; though the British administration was at places paralysed, the movement was suspended in February 1922.

In early 1930, the Indian National Congress declared that it would now be satisfied with nothing short of complete independence (*purna swaraj*). On March 2, Gandhi addressed a letter to the Viceroy, Lord Irwin, informing him that unless Indian demands were met, he would be compelled to break the 'salt laws'.

On the early morning of March 12, with a small group of followers, Gandhiji led a march towards Dandi on the sea. They arrived there on April 5th: Gandhi picked up a small lump of natural salt, and so gave the signal to hundreds of thousands of people to similarly defy the law, since the British exercised a monopoly on the production and sale of salt. This was the beginning of the civil disobedience movement.

In 1942, Gandhiji issued the last call for independence from

British rule. On the grounds of *Kranti Maidan*, he delivered a speech, asking every Indian to lay down their life, if necessary, in the cause of freedom. He gave them this mantra, "Do or Die"; at the same time, he asked the British to 'Quit India'. After a long struggle, India got independence on 15th August 1947.

One evening, Gandhiji was late for his prayers. At 10 minutes past 5 o'clock, with one hand each on the shoulders of Abha and Manu, who were known as his 'walking sticks', Gandhiji commenced his walk towards the garden.

Gandhiji folded his hands and greeted his audience with a namaskar; at that moment, a young man came up to him took a revolver out of his pocket, and shot him three times in his chest. Bloodstains appeared over Gandhiji's white woollen shawl. His hands still folded in a greeting, Gandhiji blessed his assassin, *"He Ram! He Ram"* and left us.

■■■

Drugs– The Killer of Youth

The start of college is a new and different experience for all teenagers. They are keen to learn about their new surroundings and make new friends. Many teens are attracted to drinks, smoking and drugs to be considered as cool.

In a survey recently conducted on the abuse of alcohol, nicotine, and other harmful drugs, psychologists studied that the maximum number of teenagers involved in smoking, drinking and drugs are in the age group from fourteen to twenty.

In today's society, the pressure to drink, smoke or use drugs to fit in is all around our youth.

On the basis of survey, it was found that these teenagers drink one to two times per week because they enjoy it. They feel that it is also a chance to have fun and hang out with their friends. However, teens say they also do it out of boredom. Often, teens are anxious to find an alternative way to have fun and to escape from the 'boringness' of movies and television. For this reason, often jump at the chance together in a large group to socialise. They are willing to pay their pocket money for a cup of beer, even if they known that drinking under age is illegal.

Drinking alcohol comes with many responsibilities. These teens define 'responsible drinking' as 'having control of your actions'. In other words, teens drink as long as they know what they are doing. While drinking teenagers are often put into situations where they act irresponsible.

Teenagers are often caught driving while under the influence of alcohol. When teens get into the car, they often do not think about the consequences. There is always that one thought in the back of everyone's mind in this type of situation. They say, 'nothing' bad is going to happen. Sadly, when something does happen, most of the time the drunk driver is never the one to be injured. It is always the innocent passengers or the victims on the road.

Smoking is another large issue within the college community. Many teenagers who smoke have been smoking for a few years and started smoking at an early age. Even though most people do not agree with teens smoking, a good percentage of adults smoke cigarettes. Therefore, the influence to smoke is constantly around teens and young children. On the other hand, some teens also like to smoke socially. This usually occurs at parties or just when they feel like hanging around outside of their dorms.

Drug usage is the third huge area of abuse among students in college. The majority of these teens have tried the most common gateway drug, marijuana. Many of these teenagers said they have also tried mushrooms, ecstasy, and speed.

Peer pressure has nothing to do with their reasons for drinking, smoking, or doing drugs. They believe college is the time to live. Drinking alcohol, smoking cigarettes, and using drugs are not going to stop them from having the times of their lives. Only awareness can stop them.

■■■

Science *Vs.* Religion

Science and religion... we have always heard contradictory view points on these two. It is very difficult to choose one over the other because one is based on fact and logic, while the other is built on faith and hope. That's exactly what the creation theory is, beliefs in a superior supernatural being, whereas the Big Bang theory is faith in logic. It is difficult to judge two uniquely difficult theories because both do not hold the answers; they are merely a description of the type of person we are and what morals and priorities we have with us. Someone who is atheist, for example, will believe in the scientific version; whereas someone who has had a bad life may hold onto their hope for a being that will one day make the world better for them, and hence they will trust the theory of religion. But, it's not easy to choose between the two.

Normally, when approached with a task of choice, we will subject ourselves to view every different side to each story to make an intelligible decision based on the truth. Unfortunately, with this topic we cannot. As a student, it is solely based on our personal beliefs, but where have these beliefs evolved in the first place? As we grew with each stage in our lives, we have been influenced by an outside force. Whether it be our parents, the media, our school systems-our ideas are truly not our own. How can one make an unbiased opinion with all these factors to consider? It is impossible. I grew up as a Catholic, I went to a Catholic Church all my life, my mom whom I believe is as close to a fundamentalist as they come, taught me the Creation story, my teachers at my Catholic schools taught me the same theory and so on. Of course, I am going to believe the Creation theory, I was brainwashed to believe it, and even if it is the wrong choice, I will always believe it. Even as an older pupil with an independence and a mind of my own, I still believe this, it is my faith, I learned that it was right and hence, until my death, no one will change my opinion (unless with the answers of course!) because once it's in my mind, it will never leave.

However, there is always the logical aspect to this. As you develop your mind, you start asking yourself philosophical questions; questions that have no answer and possible answers seem to contradict one another. This is where my other sense of perception can alter my already existing theory. I think that although science has not actually begun creation, it simply continued it. I am skeptical about the Adam and Eve theory, not that I doubt God's abilities, but there are gaps in that theory too. Therefore, I think God created the universe, the plant life and the animals. He created everything. But, I think humans were not derived from dust like the Bible states. I believe God created the animals, which evolved into humans. If not that, than I believe he created apes to be the first humans but saw they were not as advanced as they could be. So, He altered them slightly and then humans were made. Possibly, Adam and Eve were the first humans to exist, the Bible states God created them last anyway. Or possibly I'm wrong. Whatever the case may be, the answer is out there, but no one will ever find it.

Life Saving Drugs– Antibiotics

Antibiotics are playing an important role in our society. Sir Alexander Fleming was a founder of antibiotics through his careful observations of 1928. Without it, many lives would have been in danger due to so many infectious diseases.

Antibiotics are chemical substances produced by various species of microorganisms and other living systems that are capable of inhibiting the growth of killing bacteria and other microorganisms, in small concentrations. These organisms can be bacteria, viruses, fungi or animals, called protozoa. A particular group of these agents is made up of drugs called antibiotics.

Antibiotics can be bacteriostatic (bacteria stopped from multiplying) or bactericidal (bacteria killed). It is believed that antibiotics interfere with the surface of bacteria cells, causing a change in their ability to reproduce.

Antibiotics are manufactured in two ways. One of them is natural. At one time, all antibiotics were made from living organisms. This process, known as biosynthesis, is still used in the manufacture of some antibiotics. Other type is synthetic.

All penicillin types have an identical chemical nucleus, called a ring. The chemical chain that is attached to the ring is different in each type. By changing the molecules of the chain, scientists devise drugs with potentially different effects on different organisms. Some of these drugs are useful in treating infections some are not.

Pharmaceutical manufacturers now use computer-generated images of the rings and experiment with an endless variety of possible chains. Researchers have developed antibiotics that allow taking the medicine once in 24 hours instead of every few hours. The newer antibiotics are also more effective against a wider range of infections than were earlier drugs. There are dozens of antibiotics. The following are in common use:

Penicillin: The various types of Penicillin make up a large group of antibacterial antibiotics.

Cephalosporin: These drugs are used for combating deep infections that occur in bones and those resulting from surgery.

Aminoglycoside: These drugs are used to treat tuberculosis, bubonic plague and other infections.

Tetracycline: Tetracyclines are effective against pneumonia, typhus and other bacteria-caused illness, but can harm the function of the liver and kidney.

Macrolide: Macrolides are often used in patients who appear to be sensitive to Penicillin.

Polypeptide: The class of antibiotics called Polypeptides is quite toxic (poisonous) and is used mostly on the surface of the skin.

Allergic reactions to antibiotics are usually seen as rashes on the skin, but severe anaemia, stomach disorders and deafness can occasionally result. It was once thought that allergic reactions to antibiotics were frequent and permanent.

But, recent studies suggest that many people outgrow their sensitivity or never were allergic. The large numbers of antibiotics that are now available offer a choice of treatment that can avoid allergy-causing drugs.

It is important to remember that all drugs can cause both wanted and unwanted effects on the body. It is a fact that all drugs have the potential to be both beneficial and harmful.

Another use of antibiotics is as additives to the feed of animals. Chickens and beef cattle can be fed with these additives for better weight gains and to speed their growth.

Current work in antibiotics is largely in the area of viruses. Although, some antiviral are available, most have toxic effects so severe that they can be used only in life-threatening diseases where the negative effects are the lesser danger.

Preliminary studies, however, are reporting success in the development of safer antiviral drugs and their use should be possible within the near future.

■■■

Nuclear Power

Nuclear Power is a source of energy that has many benefits. Nuclear energy is less expensive because it is based on uranium.

With little amount of uranium a great amount of energy can be produced. It is a reliable source to count on, as there is significant amount of it on the Earth's crust.

One important advantage is that producing energy using nuclear power does not give off greenhouse gases. Green house gases are gases like carbon dioxide and sulphur dioxide, which are contributing to the greenhouse effect or global warming.

The biggest advantage of nuclear power is the discoveries made in nuclear medicine, such as cancer therapy, CAT scan and MRI machines and the use of irradiation of food to kill bacteria.

However, unfortunately nuclear power has been used in the last hundred years for the manufacture of nuclear weapons, like A-Bombs (atomic bombs) and H-Bombs (hydrogen bombs).

Nuclear weapons are weapons of mass destruction. A single weapon is capable of destroying an entire city.

In the history of warfare, nuclear weapons have been used on two occasions, both during the days of World War II in Hiroshima when a devise called 'Little Boy' was dropped, and then three days later, one in Nagasaki, called 'Fat Man'.

It is a good idea to possess nuclear weapons if a country is a 'Super Power'. If a country feels threatened it can rely on nuclear weapons to protect them from the enemy. Examples of 'Nuclear Super Powers' are USA, Russia, United Kingdom and France.

Nuclear weapons have many disadvantages. The use of them can lead to a world crisis as every time a bomb explodes, lives of millions of people are affected. Nuclear weapons are very expensive to manufacture, even though uranium is easily accessible.

■■■

India-US Nuclear Deal

India-US Nuclear deal brought about lots of hopes and aspirations to the vast multitudes of energy starved people of India. It forged a new dynamic, vibrant, business relationship with the only super power of the planet –the US.

After the initial euphoria created by the July 18 deal, few of our intellectuals started dreaming (rightly) that India is on the verge of becoming a superpower. They fell aghast when new conditions started creeping in. The May 2nd agreement attempted to fix the goalposts and remove any kind of vague discrepancies.

With vigilant media staring straight in the eyes, stiff opposition from political parties and dynamic watchdog - nuclear scientific community putting forth periodic clarifications and suggestions, the whole of India was participating in this great public debate.... should we have it or leave it.

India is one of the countries that is part of the global endeavour to master nuclear fusion technologies along with USA, Japan, S. Korea, France, Germany and China, its part of a pioneering research in TOKMAK technologies.

Nuclear fusion energy is cheap and risk free, and environmental friendly. We are competent enough to achieve significant breakthroughs in any kind of technology if only given the time and money!

One major disadvantage of nuclear power is that it makes variable amounts of radioactive waste. This waste is causing big problems for the world storage because of its irradiation. The nuclear waste has to be stored over a hundred years and the waste remains hot for thousands of years. Some people say Nuclear energy is cheaper to make but this is not the entire truth.

Although nuclear power has many disadvantages, it is necessary as long as it is used for a good cause. The fossil fuels we are currently using for making energy are some day going to run out, so we need other sources.

If nuclear power is handled correctly, the possibility of an accident is very rare.

Nuclear Power is a good substitute to burning fossil fuels for energy, as it does not contribute to global warming.

60 Years of Independence – India's Achievements

India got freedom on 15th August 1947. Many unknown heroes risked their lives so that all of us may breathe in freedom. Achieving independence was a tremendous task. After the building of the country began in right earnest. India is heading towards major superpower in the world. During the last sixty years, India has seen many up and downs.

Typically speaking, if a person reaches 60 years of age, he is labelled as an 'Old Crippled'. One can construe the picture of a man who is bed-ridden, invalid and too old to respond to any kind of treatment. He just lay aside, cherishing its blooming youthful days or he employs his time by playing with his grandchildren, but now the things have changed.

India is a 60 years old country, but is still very young, highly energetic and is working enthusiastically towards its betterment. India was free from the clutches of British in 1947. We still remember those stalwarts who sacrificed their lives to free us from British' cage enabling us to fly freely, independently in the air. We all know and have studied umpteen numbers of times about it in our History books. We studied what all "Our Father of the Nation"– "Mahatma Gandhi" did. We all our aware of the Jallianwala Bagh tragedy and many such sacrifices.

We normally say that British ruled our country – they exploited us. But, what they have given us is unity. They united our country. However, we remained united till their time only, what happened after that? Today in most of the families the two brothers are at daggers drawn with each other. Everyone under the sun has become self-centred. We all curse British, but become eagerly excited, over-enthusiastic when we get an opportunity to go abroad, like to the Big Apple. After all, who wants to stay in a country endowed with unemployment, extreme poverty, filthiness, corruption, dowry deaths and all other social evils, but remember the case of Kiranjit Walia - who bore the virulent atrocities of her husband for 10 years, no not in a diminutive village but in a country like London. Eventually, she was free and people of London persistently protested against the government to release her, Even George Bush's wife awarded her as she emanated valour, courageousness. Her dauntless act to rescue herself was truly remarkable. She won Kudos, praises, etc. But what if the same thing would have happened in India? Remember that case of a girl who was just about to get married, her in-laws demanded dowry on the verge. As it was unbearable to see the sight of how her father was accosting, her doughty act of calling cops just after few hours when she was about to tie the nuptial knot had labeled her as the most astonishingly talented women. Though being the only incident, has instilled, infused a spirit of bravery, dauntlessness, valor into female members. Yes, India has done progress, but still the disease of discrimination between male and female still exits. After 60 years, India has got its women president Ms. Pratibha Devi Singh Patil. Now, we all assess her rule, her power what changes she is going to make. Instead of saying what has to be done, we all seriously hope that she will says let's do it.

It is the people, their power of knowledge, caliber, and perseverance that makes a country good and great... it is their highly intellectual minds, decisiveness, their open and above board dealings with others. A country is empty if there are no people. We the people form our Government; we the people rule not our lives but the whole life of our stupendous country. We the people make or mar the present, future of our country. We the people mould, shape our country in whatever manner we want to. Like a one person cannot contribute significantly towards the prosperity, success of the country in the same manner it is not in the hands of one person to change it. It is the collective responsibility of all and sundry to make a gloriously bright, radiant future and to be linked together in its weal and woe. We all know that it sounds the same and hackneyed but as a matter of fact this is the only transparent and solid truth. It is we the people only who back-bite and says bad things about our country, thus this is the major reason why our country is lacking far behind and is deprived of numerous facilities as compared to others. We all should become at home in this fact.

As our Country has attained its 60 years of Independence, we must consider what the prime ministers starting from Jawaharlal Nehru to Dr. Manmohan Singh have promised about the developments that they will do in the fields of agriculture, industry, infrastructure, education etc. and the various measures implemented towards the economic growth of our country. There longevity of speech should not reflect about the planned tasks but about the accomplished tasks - that has been the biggest achievement of our country.

Let's have a look at the visible achievements made by our country so far:

METROS: Eventually, our government has once utilised its funds in an appropriate manner. Metros have made our lives relatively easier as the gap of communication has been minimised. A person does not have to wait for hours for buses. This is indeed a big achievement, and various other metros projects, which are coming up; our country is giving business to French government, thus ameliorating our relations.

TECHNOLOGY: In terms of technology, the high emergence of mobile companies, nowadays even a scrap or a vegetable vendor possess a mobile phone. The trade of mobile phone contributes more then 50% towards our economic growth. Tata has created people's car of 1 lakh... they are some of the incredibly great achievements.

ECONOMY: With RBI reducing the interest rates, Sunil Mittal acquiring Arcelor, Tata acquiring Corus, with the emergence of SEZ zones, many foreign companies intruding into India to setup their business, is in itself a great achievement, but various pros and cons attached to it.

RESEARCH: Recently Ranbaxy lost over Pfizzer over a new drug. Scientists have discovered a new planet, a star, etc.

SPACE: India has sent a space shuttle into the space. That's a landmark!

INDO-USA DEAL: It is not an achievement till yet, as the major, intense, hot dispute going between the left and the Congress for their 123 agreement has put the deal in a state of uncertainty, in a high suspense. Prime Minister has strictly said like it or lump it. But what if the Government will dissolve and the coalition government will be formed.

ENTERTAINMENT: Shilpa Shetty winning the Big Brother Show, making herself an international personality in abroad, thus making of our country proud on British grounds is a great achievement in the entertainment field. Further, with the recent win at the Oscars, we have way to go!

EDUCATION SECTOR: In a quick recap of our 2008 budget which lays emphasis on education sector is so far in the process.

INFRASTRUCTURE: No doubt the infrastructure of our country has shown immense improvement with the emergence of highways, toll bridge, metros etc.

Achievement means things, which we have successfully acquired, attained, and obtained with our hard, honest and hearty work. As mentioned above, we all are essentially self-centred, terribly selfish human beings, we want to play because we want to make centuries, we went to shine in our lives, we want to create history by making our new records, but the day we start playing as a team, not for our individual selves, we are sure to win a world cup.

Students and young generation play an important role in the process of national development. If they are good, only then the sacrifices made by our known and unknown freedom fighters will be worthwhile. Only then, India will be happy and prosperous.

■■■

Good Leader

A good leader is the one who can get the things done by his team, with the optimum support from them. A leader should gain the support of the team, not in force. But, it should come from the heart of the team. The leader should have such motivation skills to get the support from the team. Enforcing the power to get the things done cannot work for long duration. That would make the team to work without interest, that too for small duration. We saw many autocrat leaders in the history who ruled the people as per their wish. But, they could not be successful leaders.

A democrat leader is one who takes the opinion of the people before taking any decision. That would really encourage the team members to support the leader. That would bring the feeling of involvement to the team members. But if a leader is taking his own decision without consulting the team members, and if he is just enforcing that to the team, it would really bring disobedience among team members.

In history, we have seen many democrat leaders, like Mahatma Gandhi, Nelson Mandela, Abraham Lincoln, etc. They were people who gained the support of the common people and achieved miracles. We should make them examples to follow. There is a traditional definition of management, "The management is what a manager does". But that concept is nowhere relevant. Even if applied, it won't stay for a long time. So, management should be taken as an art of getting the wholehearted support from the team to get the things done by them.

What makes a good leader?

The leadership qualities that are required to make a good leader can vary in different companies, teams and situations.

This can be illustrated in both art and modern leadership models. For example, the fact that leadership qualities are dependent on context is demonstrated in the play *'The Admirable Crichton'* and the film *'Twelve O'clock High'*.

In *'The Admirable Crichton'*, written in 1902, the Lord and butler swap their roles as leader and servant as the situation changes. On a deserted island, the butler's practical skills are essential for survival, whereas the Lord's knowledge of English politics is of no value.

In the film *'Twelve O'clock High'*, produced in 1949, as a squadron starts to suffer increasing losses during the war, the leader's people-oriented approach starts to fail. He is replaced by a dictatorial bully who turns the squadron round and restores their pride.

Leadership Styles

Some people have one style of leadership, which is fine if they can find a situation that requires that style of leadership.

Flexible leadership, however, involves being able to adapt your leadership style according to the situation and the state of the team, like taking charge when a team is forming, but playing the role of coach when a team is managing itself well.

Perspective

How you approach leadership qualities will depend on whether you are looking at the subject from the perspective of an organisation or an individual.

Organisations aim to improve their performance by selecting and developing individual potential. At the outset, the needs of the organisation are usually well defined but the individuals, who may become leaders, are unknown. The organisational task is, therefore, one of:

- identifying the profile of people who will enhance organisational performance
- selecting individuals whose character, skills and potential closely match that profile
- developing those individuals so their potential becomes a reality

That is, an organisation develops a framework to assess people and develop those who are chosen.

An individual's perspective, however, is very different: the aim is for the individual to develop into a position of leadership. You are who you are, and if your profile does not fit that of the organisation you are working for, then your task is to:

- understand your own attributes or potential
- find a new role or organisation where your profile will be valued

Conclusion

Finally, what makes a good leader? The answer depends on the context. A person who can motivate a team, bend it together, lead the members to a common goal, and achieve something good, can be called a good leader.

■■■

Dowry System

Dowry is derived from the ancient Hindu customs of 'kanyadan' and 'stridhan'. In 'kanyadan', the father of the bride offers the father of the groom money or property, etc. whereas for 'stridhan', the bride herself gets jewelry and clothes at the time of her marriage, usually from her relatives or friends. In 'varadakshina', the father of the bride presents the groom cash or kind. All of these could be done voluntarily and out of affection and love.

The Hindu marriage system is sacramental. According to this system, a marriage is forever and there is no scope for a separation. Among the various ceremonies previously practiced, the ceremony in front of a 'godly' fire ('Yajna' in Sanskrit) has taken over, the old-fashioned system of marrying a wife by capture. This form of marriage began the practice of dowry, where originally, the family of the bride would accept gifts and money from the groom's family as an alternative to bloodshed during the capture of the bride. A later modification of this system has paved way for the present dowry system primarily practiced by the society.

The dowry custom continues to rule our society. In majority of Indian families, the boy has legacy rights, while the girl is given a large sum at the time of her marriage in lieu of the government regulated equal rights for girls in parental property. Thus, dowry system has spread in almost all parts of the country and sections of society. There are several reasons for the occurrence of the dowry system, but the main one is that it is a necessary precondition for marriage. 'No dowry, no marriage' is a widespread fear. There has also been an appearance of a feudal mindset with a materialistic attitude in a new globalised economy. The price tag for the groom is now bigger and bolder. The emergence of an affluent middle class, the torchbearer of social change in modern India, is the main factor for the continuation of the dowry system.

Families arrange most marriages, and a man who does not marry for love; he can marry for wealth. For this man and his family, a woman becomes the ticket to shortcut riches through the system of dowry. There are a number of things people desire to have in their own houses but cannot afford; they use the opportunity of a son's marriage to get them. The girl's parents do not protest against variety, as they regard the union as a stepping-stone towards higher social status and better matches for the remaining children. Dowry as a phenomenon has gone beyond the ritual of marriage. Pregnancy, childbirth and all kinds of religious and family functions are occasions when such demands are made. A more sophisticated public image of an extended gifting session has replaced the old system.

Now there is demand for receptions in marriage places. The trousseau includes designer wear for the bride and groom's family. Chefs are flown in for multi-cuisine wedding dinners. The bride's family usually pays for all this. The rich revel in the exchange of their black money, but this in turn exerts pressure on the other classes to ape them with serious social consequences. The women have become a kind of commodity. It is them who are the worst sufferers because dowry is most often a monetary agreement between two men – the bride's father and the groom. Caste-based practices have only added fuel to the fire. Marriages in political families are arranged to consolidate the caste base for support in electoral politics, so they do not challenge the dowry system. Dowry rituals have now spread even to communities where they were unknown. It has gone to different castes, crossed the boundaries of provinces and education and religion. Muslims and Christians, such as the Syrian Christians of Kerala and the Roman Catholics of Mangalore have started demanding dowry.

Official statistics show a steady rise in dowry crimes. More and more women are killed every year in India for dowry. Bihar and Uttar Pradesh still record the maximum number of dowry crimes, but Bangalore, India's fastest growing city also shows an alarming rise – four women reportedly die every day because of dowry harassment and domestic violence. The cases of dowry torture are the highest accounting for 32.4% of crimes against women in the country.

The Dowry Prohibition Act, in force since 1st July 1961, was passed with the purpose of prohibiting the demanding, giving and taking of dowry. In 1980, the Government setup a committee that recommended amendments in the Dowry Prohibition Act and also suggested expanding the definition of dowry and instituting family courts and National Commission for women. Many parliamentary debates led to some amendments in 1983,1984 and 1986. To stop the offences of cruelty by husband or his relatives on the wife, Section 498-A was added in the Indian Penal Code and Section 198-A in the Criminal Procedure Code in the year 1983. The Dowry Prohibition Act clearly stipulates that a person who gives or takes or helps in the giving or taking of dowry can be sentenced to jail for 5 years and fined Rs.15,000/- or the amount of the value of dowry, whichever is more. The Act also prohibits the giving and taking directly or indirectly any property or valuable security, any amount either in cash of kind, jewelry, articles, properties, etc. in respect of a marriage.

The control is provided by stating a limit and names of people gifting and their relationship to the married couple to be signed by both sides of parents.

In 1986, the Act was amended again, empowering State governments to appoint Dowry Prohibition Officers, who not only had a preventive role but also had powers to collect evidence against people who took dowry.

Despite protest by women's organisations, serious activism, legal amendments, special police cells for women, media support and heightened awareness of dowry being a crime, the practice continues unabated on a massive scale. Despite every stigma, dowry continues to be the signature of marriage. Women need real social, political, financial and moral support in their fight against the system. They have to be empowered so that they can take their decisions about their own life by refusing the dowry system.

■■■

Indian Women

In Indian society, the status of women has changed from time to time - Their position in society is the index to the standard of social organisation. We can divide the past in to three phases to analyse the status of women. They are: Ancient India, Medieval India and post-Medieval period.

Ancient Indian Women

In ancient India, women enjoyed equal status with man in all fields of life. She received the same education like man, many Hindu religious books like Vedas, Upanishads, Ramayana, Mahabharata have mentioned the names of several women who were great scholars, poets, philosophers of the time. The wife was 'Ardhangini', which means she is half of her husband. An unmarried man was considered to be incomplete. All religious ceremonies were performed by the husband along with the wife. This shows the importance given to the women in ancient period.

Medieval Period Indian Women

However, in the medieval period, the status of women went down considerably. She was considered to be inferior to man. Many historians have called this age as the 'dark age'. Her position became very miserable. Decline in the status of women in Indian society begins with the Muslims rule in India: customs of purdha, sati, child marriage and restrictions on widow marriage become prevalence of joint family system. They were the major factors responsible for the injustice done towards women. These problems related with women resulted in changed mindset of people. They began to consider a girl as misery and a burden, which had to be secured from the eyes of intruders and needed extra care. All this gave rise to some new evils, such as child marriage, sati, jauhar and restriction on girl education

Sati: The ritual of dying at the funeral pyre of the husband is known as 'Sati' or 'Sahagaman'. According to some of the Hindu scriptures, women dying at the funeral pyre of her husband go straight to heaven. So it was considered good to practice this ritual. Sati was considered to be a better option then living as a widow as the plight of widows in Hindu society was even worse.

Jauhar: It is also more or less similar to Sati, but it is a mass suicide. Jauhar was prevalent in the Rajput societies. In this custom, wives immolated themselves while their husband were still alive. When people of Rajput clan became sure that they were going to die at the hands of their enemy, then all the women arranged a large pyre and set themselves afire.

Child Marriage: It was a norm in medieval India. Girls were married off at the age of 8-10. They were not allowed access to education and were treated as material beings. The child marriage along with it brought some more problems such as increased birth rate, poor health of women due to repeated child bearing and high mortality rate of women and children.

Restriction on Widow Remarriage: The condition of widows in medieval India was very bad. They were not treated as human beings and were subjected to a lot of restrictions. They were supposed to live pious life after their husband died and were not allowed entry in any celebration.

Purdah System: The veil or the 'Purdah' system was widely prevalent in medieval Indian society. It was used to protect the women folk from the eyes of foreign rulers who invaded India in medieval period. But, this system curtailed the freedom of women.

Girl Education: The girls of medieval India and especially Hindu society were not given formal education. They were given education related to household chores.

Though these evils were present in medieval Indian society, they were mainly confined to Hindu society. As compared to Hindu society, other societies such as Buddhism, Jainism and Christians were a bit lenient. Women in those societies enjoyed far more freedom. The status of women in Southern India was better than the North India. While in Northern India there were not many women administrators, in Southern India we can find some names that made women of that time proud. There was one major evil present in South India of medieval time. It was the custom of Devadasis.

Devadasis was a custom prevalent in Southern India. In this system, girls were dedicated to temples in the name of gods and goddesses. All the requirements of Devadasis were fulfilled by the grants given to the temples. In the temple, they used to spend their time in the worship of god and by singing and dancing for the god. Some kings used to invite temple dancers to perform at their court for the pleasure of courtiers, and thus, some Devadasis converted to Rajadasis (palace dancers) prevalent in some tribes of South India, like Yellamma cult.

Women's Struggle and Reforms

Though women of India were not at par with her counterpart in Western world but she started struggling hard to make her mark in man's world. We can count on certain names from the British India where women put the example of extraordinary bravery which even men might not be able to show. Rani Lakshmi Bai of Jhansi was the one such woman. There have many social reformers who helped women gain their previous status in society.

Raja Ram Mohan Roy - He was strictly against the evils prevalent in society in his time. He is the one who has done women a great favour by abolishing Sati lawfully. Ram Mohan Roy also did great work in the field of women education. He was against child marriage and favoured widow remarriage.

Ishwar Chandra Vidyasagar - Ishwar Chandra Vidyasagar was popularly known as Vidyasagar, which means 'sea of knowledge'. He strongly supported women education in Bengal and went door to door to persuade people to send their girl child to school. He also did a lot in the field of widow remarriage. He opened many schools for girls.

Mahatma Jyotirao Phule - He was the one to open first girl school in India. He is also credited with opening first home for widows of the upper caste and a home for newborn girl children so that they can be saved from female infanticide.

Swami Dayananda Saraswati - He emphasised for the equal rights for women in every field. He tried to change the mindset of people with his Vedic teachings.

Mahatma Gandhi - He was the one who liberated Indian women from the clutches of 'Purdah' and other social evils.

Post-Medieval Period

The status of women in modern India is a sort of a irony. If on one hand she is at the peak of ladder of success, on the other hand she is suffering the violence afflicted on her by her own family members. As compared with past, women in modern times have achieved a lot, but in reality they still have to travel a long way. Their path is full of roadblocks. The women have left the secured domain of their home and are now in the battlefield of life, fully armored with their talent. There are many problems which women in India have to go through daily. These problems have become the part and parcel of life of Indian women and some of them have accepted them as their fate.

The main problems of Indian women includes:

Malnutrition - Generally in India, women are the one who eat last and least in the whole family. So they eat whatever is left after men folk are satiated. As a result, most of the times their food intake does not contain the nutritional value required in maintaining the healthy body. In villages, sometimes women do not get to eat the whole meal due to poverty.

Poor Health - The malnutrition results in poor health of women. The women of India are prejudiced from the birth itself. They are not breastfed for long. In the want of a son, the women wants to get pregnant as soon as possible which decreases the caring period to the girl child, whereas the male members get adequate care and nutrition.

Maternal Mortality - The mortality rate in India is among highest in the world, as females are not given proper attention, which results in the malnutrition and then they are married at an early age which leads to pregnancies at younger age when the body is not ready to bear the burden of a child. All this results in complications, which may lead to gynecological problems, which may become serious with time and may ultimately, lead to death.

Lack of Education - In India, women education never got its due share of attention. The people of villages consider girls to be a curse and they do not want to waste money and time on them, as they think that women should be wedded off as soon as possible.

Mistreatment - In India, violence against women is a common evil. Not just in remote parts, but in cities also, women bear the brunt. They are subjected to physical and mental violence.

Overworked - Indian women work more than men of India but their work is hardly recognised as they mainly do unskilled work. Their household chores is never counted as a work, if a woman is working in a field to help her husband it will also be not counted as a work.

Lack of Power - In India a large percentage of women do not have power. They cannot take decisions independently, not even related to their own life. They have to take permission of male members for each and every issue. They don't have any say in important household matters and not in matter of their own marriage.

Marriage - The family mainly fixes the marriages in India. The scenario in villages is very bad. Going against the wishes of husband is considered to be a sin. In a marriage, the husband always has the upper hand.

Dowry - Courts are flooded with cases related to death due to dowry harassment by husband and in laws. Due to this evil practice, many newly wed women of India have to lose their lives.

Female Infanticide - As women were supposed to be and in some areas of India are still considered to be curse by some strata of society. Their birth is still taken as a burden. A pregnant woman is often forced to abort her child if it is discovered that the child is a girl.

Divorce - It is regarded as the sign of failure of marriage, especially of women. She is treated as if she has committed some crime by divorcing her husband.

Current Scenario - However, the position of women in modern India has changed considerably. Her position in modern Indian society is equal to that of men, socially, economically, educationally, politically and legally. Now, she has the right to receive education, inherit own property, participate in public life and political life of the nation. She has become economically independent. She can seek employment anywhere and remain not a domestic slave. She is certainly enjoying the equal status with man in many Indian states.

Some Bright Spots

- India has world's largest number of professionally qualified women.
- India has largest population of working women in the world.
- India has more number of doctors, surgeons, scientists, and professors than the United States

Women Achiever

Today Indian women have excelled in each and every field from social work to visiting space station. There is no arena, which has remained unconquered by Indian women. Whether it is politics, sports, entertainment, literature, or technology, everywhere we can hear applauses for her.

Politics

Women of India are highly active today in this area. Sarojini Naidu, Vijaylakshami Pandit, Sucheta Kriplani were the torchbearer for the women of India. Shrimati Vijay Lakshami Pandit was the first Indian woman to hold a post in the cabinet.

The most important name in the category of women politicians of recent times is Mrs. Indira Gandhi. Today, her daughter-in law Mrs. Sonia Gandhi is following her footsteps and leading the Indian National Congress. Other women who have made their name in politics of India are Shiela Dixit, Uma Bharti, Jayalalitha, Vasundhra Raje and Mamata Banerjee.

Sports

Indian women have achieved great laurels for the nation in every sport. Whether it is cricket or hockey, India has national women team for every game. Indian women cricket team has won Asia Cup of 2004 and 2005 and made country proud. Some women sports icons of India are:

- P.T. Usha (Athletics)
- Kunjarani Devi (Weight lifting)
- Diana Edulji (Cricket)
- Sania Mirza (Tennis)
- Karnam Malleshwari (Weight lifting)

Art and Entertainment

This area is full of Indian women. We have many names to boast of, like M.S. Subbulakshmi, Indian Nightingale Lata Mangeshkar, Asha Bhosle, as famous singers; Madhu Bala, Rekha, Aishwarya Rai as Bollywood queens. Today, Indian woman is a painter, an actor, a singer, and a beauty queen.

Literature

Arundhati Roy, Anita Desai, Kiran Desai, Shobhaa De, Jhumpa Lahiri are famous names in Indian literature. Not just in India, today these women are recognised all over the world. Arundhati Roy has been awarded with the Booker Prize of 1997 for her work 'God of Small Things'. Kiran Desai has been given Booker Prize of 2006 and Jhumpa Lahiri got recognition in the form of Pulitzer Prize.

Corporate Divas

Kiran Majumdar Shaw is the undisputed corporate queen of India. She is the richest Indian woman. Another names in this list include Vidya Mohan Chhabaria, Chairperson of Jumbo Group, Naina Lal Kidwai, Vice Chairperson and Managing Director of HSBC Securities and Capital Market, Sullaijja Firodia Motwani and Mallika Srinivasan.

Social Saints

The Indian saint of today's times Mother Teresa is the name which every Indian whether rich or poor is familiar with. Another important names working for the cause of people includes Aruna Roy who worked for the save RTI Campaign and Medha Patekar who is associated with Narmada Bachao Andolan.

Universal Queens

Kalpana Chawla, who was the member of Colombia Space Shuttle, which exploded on its way back, was the first Indian woman astronaut who visited space station. And now, following on her footsteps another women of Indian origin Sunita Williams has become the second one to be the member of International Space Station crew.

Indian women have mastered anything and everything which a woman can dream of. But, she still has to go a long way to achieve equal status in the minds of Indian men.

■■■

Terrorism

Terrorism is the systematic use of terror or unpredictable violence against governments, publics, or individuals, to attain a political objective. It evolved from numerous attacks in the 20th century, to less frequent but more destructive result in the 21st century.

In the 20th century, terrorism went through some great changes. The use of new technology such as automatic weapons and electrically bursting explosives encouraged terrorists to act violently and provided them with an easier way of attacking. At the time, attacks were mainly from groups trying to undermine or overthrow existing political institutions. However, today terrorism exists with different causes and purposes in mind. It has been used in anti-colonial conflicts such as in Ireland, Britain, Algeria and France. It is used when settling conflicts between different groups in possession of homeland such as Palestine and Israel. It is also used in religious disagreements in the case of the Catholics and Protestants in Northern Ireland and in internal conflicts between revolutionary forces and established governments, for example: Malaysia, Argentina, Iran, and Nicaragua.

Terrorism went from numerous attacks in the 20th century, to less frequent but more destructive assaults in the 21st century. The threat of terrorism has now become more deadly. But, the freedom fighters as some people call themselves, are fighting back with no mercy. Over the past couple of years, terrorists have developed new tactics such as portable bombs, suicide operatives, and weapons of mass destruction. These have been known to result in hundreds, not to say thousands of people being injured or killed. Some people even become terrorist, or are forced into terrorising for reasons that they do not even know. As Michael Herr mentions, "Every day people were dying because of some small detail that they couldn't be bothered to observe." Take September 11, 2001 into consideration, when two airplanes were hijacked and crashed into the World Trade Centre and another into the pentagon. In just two hours, families were torn apart, courage was tested, and the world was shaken forever. The hijackers had probably believed that they were dying on that plane for their country, but sadly did not know the true and exact reason for their presence, or their life for that matter. At the Democratic National Convention, Hillary Clinton said, "I visited Ground Zero right after we were attacked. I felt like I was standing at the Gates of Hell. I hope no American ever has to witness a sight like that again."

Even India is facing a problem of terrorism. It is a bit unfortunate that we as a country are facing hostilities from our neighbouring countries since independence. Pakistan, since its creation, has always harboured terrorist elements against India with an intention to destabilise our country. China, the Big Brother, supports Pakistan in their endeavour to divide India. We face threats from Bangladesh and from Sri Lanka in the South. Since we have open borders with Nepal, terrorists use Nepal as easy entry and exit points. Our borders with Pakistan and Bangladesh are porous and not fully sealed. We face trouble on the North-East side with China claiming Arunachal Pradesh. These countries hobnob with these terrorists and have helped them to establish their bases from where they can carry out their evil acts. So, all the expertise for planting Bombs on soft targets come from these countries. But, not everything can be done from these foreign bases. So, they take advantage of the unemployed youth and others who fall easy prey to their indoctrination and create local groups who create trouble in all cities across India. They take help from some political class and the corrupt officials provide fodder for their entry and exit from India.

Terrorism is not about Muslims only and their quest for Jihad. Not all Muslims are terrorists and not all terrorists are Muslims. India's 140 million Muslims are a salutary negation of the facile thesis about Islam's incompatibility with democracy. The terrorists that we encounter today are not men who commit evil acts out of revenge. For these men indoctrinated by outfits like the Al Qaeda and the Dawood gangs, terrorism is a full-fledged profession. The cold-blooded killers of Ahmedabad went about with their tasks with clinical precision. They did it because it was a job they wanted to do. Only few Muslims believe that these phonies are fighting for any cause but their own. Hindus have stopped fulminating against terror despite the heavy toll it takes each time. For these terrorists who are invisible, they have no agenda. They do it in the name of Jihad or some linguistic or religious cause, which a common man does not identify himself with.

India earned its reputation as a soft state that can be intimidated into meeting terrorists' demands. Our foreign minister in the year 1999 in the month of December personally escorted three terrorists freed by India in order to secure the release of passengers of a hijacked Indian Airlines flight to Taliban controlled Afghanistan. This act led to the 9/11 attack in New York, as one of these very terrorists was later implicated in the 9/11 attacks. Tough rhetoric and reactive government policies and Draconian acts like the POTA will not serve the cause for curbing such terrorism. It will only result in violation of human rights and engineer more youth to fall prey to such terrorist organisations. We have to break out of this trap that we have imposed on ourselves.

Democratic politics, political freedoms, civil liberties and religious tolerance must be protected at all costs. The corruption and politicisation of the police forces must be minimised. We need a dedicated and an unbiased police force. Criminalisation of politics must stop. Instead, we have number of parliamentarians with pending criminal cases. Some jailed parliamentarians also cast their vote on important National issues, which is alarming! Terrorism prospers and thrives in such conditions. In a way, Poverty is an incubator of terrorism and a root cause of corruption. It breeds the Naxalites and the local terrorist groups. The government needs to be tough in implementing reforms to maintain rapid economic growth and uplift the status of its downtrodden people.

More importantly, India's terrorism problem is largely specific to Kashmir. There is a difference between terrorists and freedom fighters and one should not equate them. India must muster international support in this issue and put pressure on Pakistan to stop supporting these terrorists. India habitually points fingers at Pakistan, which is the hotbed and the epicentre of terrorism all around the world. But, merely pointing fingers will not help matters. For a small country like Pakistan to be able to infiltrate groups of Indians and recruit them to the terrorist's cause indicates failures of the intelligence on the other hand. We have to look into this fact. There is no co-ordination between the central intelligence agencies and the states. Each points a finger at others each time a bomb blast takes place. This is matched by the flaws of the criminal justice system, which is rudimentary by the standards of mature democracies. Whether it is the Bombay bomb blasts of 1992 or the Gujarat riots in 2002, justice takes many years to deliver. Justice has neither been done, nor seen to be done. India needs to be tough but not reactionary to the causes of terrorism.

■■■

Indian Sports

Sports and physical education are necessary components of human development, good health, and companionship and to have a spirit of friendly competition. This has a positive impact on the overall development of the personality. Brilliance in sports enhances a person's sense of achievement, national pride and patriotism. Sports in India include both indoor games like chess, snooker, and playing cards and outdoor games like football, cricket, badminton and tennis.

Traditional Sports in India

Sports in India dates back to the ancient times with references found in the Vedas and Indus Valley Civilisation. Archaeological excavations of Mohenjodaro and Harappa reveal that people indulged in some sort of physical activities and also played a variety of games using marbles, balls and dice. Hunting, swimming, boating and boxing were also some of the major sports played and nurtured in India in ancient times.

Yoga was an integral part of ancient Indian culture. Yoga was practice by almost every school thought to achieve spiritual and mental peace. The people forgot it but now people have once again realised the importance of yoga.

The present scenario of coaches is also a part of traditional sports. The guru–shishya trend or the teacher–pupil relationship can be traced back to the times of *Ramayana* and *Mahabharata*. The gurus would take their shihyas under their custody and introduce them to archery, chariot racing, wrestling, hunting, horse riding, weight lifting, swimming and military tactics. The weapons of war, for instance, the javelin (toran) and the discus (chakra), were frequently used in sports.

Games like chess, snakes and ladders, playing cards, polo, the martial arts of judo and karate had originated in India and it was from here that these games were transmitted to foreign countries, where they were further developed.

Chess originated in ancient India and was known as Chaturanga – meaning four limbs. It represents four-fold division on the ancient Indian army – infantry, war elephants, cavalry and chariots. Chaturanga is the direct ancestor of shatranj, which was played by the Pandavas and the Kauravas.

The popular game of cards originated in ancient India and was known as Krida-patram. It was one of the favourite pastimes of Indians in ancient times. This game was patronised especially by the royalty and nobility. In medieval India, playing cards was known as Ganjifa cards which were played in practically all royal courts.

Ancient India claims to have been the origin of judo and karate. Kerala's martial art form Kalaripayate is similar to karate. Those who practice it have to develop acrobatic capabilities, when using swords or knives to attack their adversaries, and even an unarmed exponent who can be a force to reckon with.

Popular Sports in Present India

Hockey - Hockey is the national game of India. It has made India stand tall and has proved itself to the world, in spite of being under political suppression. Hockey is a team game, which is played by two teams of eleven players. Either team tries to hit the ball with the hockey stick into the goal, and also tries to prevent the opponent from doing so. The game of hockey is played widely across India. It is popular and is played by both men and women. The origins of the game can be traced back to the earliest civilisations of the world. The rules of hockey are very similar to the rules of football except that players must use sticks instead of their feet to play the ball.

Cricket - Cricket is a team game, which is played between two teams of eleven players each. It's a bat-and-ball game. In India, cricket is by far the most popular sport and almost practiced like a religion. The cricket field consists of a large circular or oval-shaped grassy ground. The pitch where the batsmen have to face the bowler is 22 yards. The objective of the game is to score more runs than the opposing team. The team bowling first tries to bowl out the batting side, and then out score them. Batting and bowling are thus alternated.

Tennis - Tennis is the game in which two opposing players (singles) or pairs of players (doubles) use tightly strung rackets to hit a ball of specified size, weight, and bounce over a net on a rectangular court.

Points are awarded to a player or team whenever the opponent fails to correctly return the ball within the prescribed dimensions of the court. One of the distinguishing factors, which make tennis more special among all other sports, is its simplicity of rules. A player's objective is to make the opponent discontinue the rally.

Football - Football is considered to be the most popular sport in India. It is also a team sport played between two teams of 11 players each. It is a ball game played on a rectangular grass field with a goal post at each end. The object of the game is to score by maneuvering the ball into the opposition's goal post. The team who scores the maximum number of goals is the winner. The rules of football are quite simple; you have to use your foot to guide the ball and pass it within your teammates and score a goal.

River rafting - River rafting is done using a raft on whitewater or different degrees of rough water, in order to have some thrill and excitement. In India, one can enjoy river rafting on the Ganges. The Ganga near Rishikesh in Uttarakhand is a popular spot for whitewater rafting. The whitewater river rafting stretch of the Ganges is from Kaudiyala to Rishikesh where the river has 12 major rapids over 36-kms long, most of which are easily navigable.

Scuba diving and snorkeling - They are done using self-contained breathing equipment to stay underwater for periods of time greater than human breath-holding ability allows. The diver swims underwater using fins attached to the feet.

If one wants to dive into the water to check out the beautiful marine life hidden inside the mysterious horizons of the sea, then the coastal regions of India are the best places for divers and snorkellers.

Surrounded by a long stretch of coastal belt on the three sides, a water sport fan can get immense opportunities in India to enjoy the sun, sand, sea and surf.

Canoeing and Kayaking - Canoeing and kayaking are other popular water sports in India. The facilities for these sports are available along the beaches of Indian coastline and lakes of north India and northeastern states of India. To move on the cool blue waters, brings loads of thrill to the adventurer.

Rock climbing - It is a sport in which a person loves to climb a steep rock. People use gears and safety equipments while climbing.

This is a physically exhausting sport and is very much challenging. Manali Valley in Uttar Pradesh is an excellent place for rock climbing.

Trekking - This includes walking through the mountains and exploring some of the hidden cultures and living styles of India. Just walk through mountains and streams.

Some of the other adventure sports in India are paragliding, skating, skiing and rappelling.

One can also visit the forests and deserts and enjoy the animal's safari, jeep safari and stay in the camps.

Now days, government is also promoting sports by different means. Sports awards are given by the Sports Ministry of India to honour the players who have performed very well in their field of sport. It is done so as to enhance the player's spirit and recognise his or her achievements. It is also intended to help and support sportspersons with outstanding caliber. In future, India will also have name in the world of sports.

■■■

Co-education

Co-education is the recent system of education where girls sit and study along with boys in the same class and in a common college or school. This system was not popular in ancient schools and colleges. At that time, it was not considered appropriate to allow boys and girls to study together in same institutions. Rather, boys and girls were sent to separate schools and colleges. Social mixing of boys and girls was not allowed. This was considered essential to maintain the purity of character in them.

Actually, the elders of each family consider many disadvantages in co-education and that's why they are against sending their children or grand-children to such schools and colleges. They think that co-education makes their children absent-minded. The children become indisciplined and the whole environment of the schools and colleges gets polluted.

The boys try all sorts of motions, gestures and songs to attract the attention of the girls. Even the girls tempt the boys for all sorts of indiscipline. Boys do not come for the teachers in the class. They keep combing their hair off and on and waste their time and energy. The boys and girls all try to show themselves as heroes and heroines respectively and are mostly running to cinemas to see latest movies. The educational institutions start presenting a look of fashion parades. All sorts of unsocial and undesirable habits are developed and students forget to listen to their elders or teachers. In such an environment, one cannot expect a good quality character.

However, if carried under certain restrictions, co-education is considered better from social point of view in spite of its various defects as explained above. Such a system of education gives an opportunity to understand each other's problems and, therefore, can co-operate better in achievement of respective goals. A healthy spirit of working and competing is created by co-education.

The boys try to keep a polite and gentle character so as to give a good impression to their girls class-fellows. During their long period of education, they can better understand each other's psychology and even can choose their life partners from among their class-fellows.

In this way, the problem of parents to select a suitable match for their children is also solved. The boy and girl educated together make the best match due to their broad attitude towards life and closer understanding of each other's habits and manners of living, likes and dislikes.

Co-education provides economical and advanced education to girl students. This is because the same amount of money is invested to upgrade or provide better equipments and infrastructure in schools and colleges. Otherwise, funds would get diverted for constructing separate schools and colleges for girls.

Further, in a free democratic country like India, we cannot deny education to girls along with boys; the girls must also be equally educated.

However, where girl students take interest in greater numbers towards studies, there, special separate institutions can be established to impart education of each level and in various professions.

The history of co-education in India has been of mixed kind, in the northern part of our country; there are a large number of co-educational schools. While in the southern part the number of unisex schools are more. This is also true for the rural India, where the rural masses upon both the boys and girls studying together.

However, many people who do not favour this system of education are of the opinion that this system is not good. They feel that co-education is an urban phenomenon. They give reasons like the boys and girls are different from each other. They feel that since men have to earn for the family and women have to look after the household, their education should not be on similar lines.

On the contrary, people who favour this system believe it to be good because they feel that both girls and boys have to face the same situation when they grow up. They have to struggle to find good jobs.

They have to perform the same functions inside and outside their homes besides studying together gives birth to healthy relations. Boys become more polite and gentle in the presence of girls, while girls become bold and confident in the company of boys.

Another advantage of a co-educational school is that the expenditure on setting up two sets of schools. This saves precious resources for other development purposes. Boys and girls more expressive, progressive and forward in outlook and attitude to life, which can be of great advantage to both sexes.

Co-education seems to be good at primary level and higher level in colleges. But, due care must be taken at high school and inter-classes where lot of physical and mental changes take place naturally in children.

Students must be guided properly to avoid their going

astray. Separation between girls and boys can be made taking them into confidence and making them understand any implications.

As such, at high school level, co-education can be imparted with able guidance and care. At university level, boys and girls get matured to understand good or bad of each other. So, co-education can be very useful from social and economic point of view if given under proper care and guidance.

When one analyses these factors, one comes to a conclusion that the advantages of co-education outweigh their disadvantages.

■■■

Generation Gap

Generation gap is the gap between the world of the adult and the world of the youth. This gap has existed ever since parents and children existed. Youth have their own thinking beliefs and customs and adults have their own beliefs and customs. The adults don't understand the world of the youth and are antagonistic to what ever the youth do and the communication between the adult and the youth comes to a standstill.

Thus, there is a rift between the adult and the youth. When the child becomes a teenager he is curious about every thing and he also wants to know why. The child who never questioned the authority of the parent till now starts questioning the parent. The parents are disappointed. The child begins to think critically. The parents who are upset with the child were alsc the one who opposed their parents when they were teenager. Yet, they doesn't understand his child.

The adult always follows the customs set by their elders and don't want to change it and even can't think of changing it. But the youth tries to put some scientific reasoning for those customs.

This leads to arguments between them and there is clash of ideas. The youth think of adult as silly and the adult thinks of the youth as being rude and disobedient. The adult cannot accept the fact that his child has got his own independent thoughts. The parents won't like their children going to parties and spending more time outside.

The youth are attracted to fashion and the customs of the

west and try to ape the west, which the adults despise. So, the adult don't like the way the youth dress, their mode of living and all the activities and keep criticising them and objecting them on every move. The youth feels controlled and restricted. They feel that the adults are like blocks to their happiness and at times feels to run away from home. Mostly girls are victims of criticism. The older women backbite against the girl for talking to a boy or about the dress she wears. She gets emotionally disturbed. Most girls and boys are victims of a scandals.

The scientific and technological innovations have totally transformed the environment for the present generation as compared to previous generation. The developments in technology, especially communication and transportation, have totally transformed the life of this generation.

This generation has access to a wide range of electronic gadgets making their life more and more comfortable. The emergence of fast foods has made their life much more easier. But those who can afford to have these modern technology could make their lives totally different from their previous generations.

But, for another set of people, it only forced their simmering frustration. Exposure to luxurious life-styles has increased, but their ability to meet these new found aspirations remained dull over generations.

As a result, there is a clear disobedient tendency in the present generation whereas the earlier generation more prepared to accept their difficulties.

The social separation and unfriendliness have become the harsh features of this generation. A sense of community feeling and community effort have been replaced by a penchant to get things done on their own and in their interest by hook or crook. Social togetherness has become a casualty as relations have become impersonal. This feature is much move striking in the nightmarious metropolitan life.

This social separation and unfriendliness is resulting in a phenomenon of increasing crime rate, levels of frustration and diffusion of energies of the youth on destructive lines.

No society can prosper without properly understanding and appreciating the past, analysing the present in the light of past experiences and shaping the future by combining the wisdom of the present and the past.

But, the greatest calamity that is going to happen for Indian society will be due to this generation's increasing lack of sense of history. As a result, the patriotic favour seen in the Japanese or Chinese youth is obviously missing in Indian youth today.

However, the generations have changed over the attitude towards man-made barriers in society.

In fact, these barriers have became much wider in the present generation than the previous ones. The brotherhood and love that kept the society united throughout the generations are fading away. The earlier generations were fired by zealous nationalism and saw their individual destiny with that of overall nation's destiny. This is not to ignore the exceptions. Exceptions exist for every trend then and now.

This gap between the adult and youth exists in every generation. It's not that difficult to bridge the gap between the adult and the youth. The gap between the adult and youth can be bridged by

1. The adult should give more independence to the youth.

2. Trust should be maintained.
3. Both should discuss things openly and in a friendly manner.
4. Understanding and trying to understand is more important.
5. Adults have to accept some changes.
6. Both should respect each other and come to a compromise.
7. The youth also should behave in a responsible manner and respect the views of the adult even though he doesn't follow it.

The youth will become an adult one day and the adult was also a youth once. So, both of them should treat each other with respect

Indian society presents a contrasting picture. For a vast majority, life continues to be a struggle for generations together. The gap only that exists for them is the gap between their means and needs. They find it increasingly difficult to make both the ends meet. For the middle classes, the gap is between their means and ballooning aspirations. The affluent and upper middle classes find this generation gap as a pleasant experience.

Certainly this generation is fortunate to have greater opportunities. Scientific and technological innovations have made seemingly impossible things possible. These innovations have also radically transformed the life of the present generations. But, the society can forge ahead into future by analysing the present in the light of the past. In the rapidly changing current environment, gap between generations is usual.

But, a leapfrogging may prove to be counter productive. The gap should be towards the positive end.

As we know, the fact of life is on and after every 5 years there is a new generation that stands up to compete us and that makes a generation gap. This has been seen every moment that generation gap raises a friction between previous and current, it should not be acceptable. The new generation is like a garden of soft flowers and the previous are gardener. So, with this regard, they need our proper care and guidance to bloom and spread their beauty. We are not going or being old in front of next generation, but we are more experienced against them.

Every time a generation gap is shown, we would have to minimise it. We have to run with time. The future of citizens and nations depend on the generation crops. So, we need to give them proper harvest and care.

■■■

HIV - AIDS

HIV stands for Human Immunodeficiency Virus. It is the virus that causes AIDS. A member of a group of viruses called retroviruses, HIV infects human cells and uses the energy and nutrients provided by those cells to grow and reproduce.

AIDS stands for Acquired Immunodeficiency Syndrome. It is a disease in which the body's immune system breaks down and is unable to fight off infections, known as 'opportunistic infections' and other illnesses that take advantage of a weakened immune system.

HIV and Aids has affected more than roughly thirty million people worldwide. India has among the highest number of persons living with HIV/AIDS in the world today, although the overall prevalence remains low. There are more than 5.1 million individuals infected with HIV in this country of over 1 billion people (UNAIDS 2003). The total number of AIDS cases in 2002 was estimated to be about 550,000. Seven states — Andhra Pradesh, Goa, Karnataka, Maharashtra, Manipur, Mizoram, and Nagaland — already have generalised epidemics, as indicated by a 1 percent or higher prevalence rate among pregnant women in prenatal clinics. These seven states represent 22 percent of the population.

It is estimated that by the end of 20th century there were 40 million people infected with HIV all over the world and India has been leading with highest number of cases (ranging from 10-20 million). We may not be infected, but will definitely be affected indirectly by it. Hence, it is a duty of every citizen of India to have detailed knowledge about this disease.

Due to lack of knowledge about AIDS people have fear in their mind against the victims of this disease. Because of fear of social boycott, AIDS patients and their relatives hide their HIV status. Many doctors (due to fear of getting infection) also refuse to treat these patients. There is danger of AIDS for everybody and only thing that can save us is to be completely informed.

How HIV Spreads

Several factors put India in danger of experiencing AIDS. These risk factors include:

Unsafe Sex and Low Condom Use: In India, sexual transmission is responsible for 84 percent of reported AIDS cases. HIV-prevalence rates are highest among sex workers and their clients, including drug users, and men who have sex with other men.

Injecting Drug Use (IDU): Studies indicate that many drug users are switching from inhaling to injecting drugs. This phenomenon is more localised in the Northeastern states of India, and injecting drug users show sharp increases in HIV prevalence.

Low Status of Women: Infection rates have been on the increase among women and infants in some states.

Widespread Stigma: Stigma towards people infected with HIV/AIDS is widespread. The misconception that AIDS only affects men who have sex with men, sex workers, and injecting drug users strengthens and perpetuates existing discrimination.

How HIV Infect

AIDS is caused by HIV, a very fragile RNA type of retrovirus, which like any other microorganism lives inside the living cells of the body. Outside body it doesn't survive for more than half an hour.

There are two types of HIV virus, i.e. HIV-1 and HIV-2. HIV-1 is present all over the world and in India more than 80% people are affected by it. HIV-2 is mainly found in Africa and also presents in India.

Some people are infected with both the viruses. People only infected with HIV-2 live longer than those infected with HIV-1 and chances of transmission of HIV-2 from mother to child are very rare.

Once in body, HIV attacks CD4 type of White Blood Cells (WBCs) in blood and gradually kills them. These CD4 type of WBC helps us to fight against various infections.

Once they are destroyed our body's resistance to fight infections goes down and person suffers from lots of infections. This end stage of HIV infection is called AIDS. It takes many years for AIDS to develop and till that time infected person usually remains healthy.

How HIV is not Transmitted

There is no risk of contracting HIV infection in daily routine activities and by casual contact with HIV positive person.

HIV virus is not transmitted through:

- Embarrassing or kissing (social)
- Touching hand shaking or hugging
- Sharing bathroom or toilet
- Coughing, saliva or sneezing
- Eating together or sharing utensils
- Swimming pools
- Sharing clothes

- Mosquito bite, Insect bite or houseflies
- Patient caring

What are the Symptoms of AIDS

An HIV infected person initially looks normal and perfectly healthy. The symptoms of AIDS develop after few years and include:

- Long standing, unexplained fever (> 1 month)
- Unexplained diarrhoea (> 1 month)
- Persistent cough (> 1 month)
- Persistent unexplained fatigue and weight loss of more than 5 kg within short period
- White blotches in the mouth or on tongue

How HIV can be Detected

You cannot tell by looking at person's face whether he or she is infected with HIV. The infected person looks perfectly healthy and feels well for years. The infection can be detected by doing a blood test i.e. ELISA HIV antibody test. If someone is found to be positive by ELISA and confirmed by second test the person is said to be seropositive.

How can HIV be Prevented

Prevention is simple easy and the only answer we have got today unless we find some cure. Adopting simple measures such as can easily prevent HIV:

Safe Sex: - The only safe sex is 'no sex'; all other practices like masturbation, cuddling, hugging, rubbing, sticking to one partner or using condom if one cannot avoid multiple partners are safer sex practices.

Safe Blood - Judicious use of blood and use only tested HIV free blood or blood product.

Safe Needles: Insist your doctors and nurses to use sterile or disposable needles and instruments.

Safe Motherhood: Before taking any major step in life like, marriage or having child, ascertain that you are HIV free.

Specific Anti-HIV Treatment: Many new anti-HIV drugs which prevent the spread of the virus available at selected places in market and few of them are also manufactured in India. But, these medicines are very costly and in India 90% of HIV patients cannot even think of them.

Government has taken many steps to aware people. Currently, the World Bank is carrying out sector work on the economic consequences of the HIV/AIDS epidemic on India and is actively supporting the design of the third National AIDS Control Programme.

There are numerous NGOs working on HIV/AIDS issues in India at the local, state, and national levels. Projects include targeted interventions with high-risk groups; direct care of people living with HIV/AIDS; general awareness campaigns; and care for AIDS orphans. Funding for NGOs comes from a variety of sources, like the federal or state governments of India, international donors, and local contributions.

Remember AIDS does not discriminate caste, creed, race, religion, and educational or social status. Prevention of AIDS is our joint responsibility. Education and awareness is the only weapon in our hand. Let us accept the challenge to fight against AIDS. We must support and care for the people with HIV/AIDS with compassion and understanding.

■■■

Fashion

Every person nurtures an innate desire of looking good and feel 'accepted' in the socio-economic circle. The word fashion instantaneously brings to mind a flash of colour with a dash of glamour. Women are taking to fashion in a big way, and are experimenting with different looks, styles, and textures.

Fashion plays an increasingly important role in an individual's life because it is considered as a means of self-expression. The garments and accessories that man or women wear, help them to identify with a group of others-whether it is a lifestyle, profession, a religion, or an attitude. Thus, the term 'fashion' has become synonymous with the overall growth of the country as well.

Several factors contribute to the evolution of fashion as a whole. It is a widely accepted fact that the rich and the famous, and the political figures and royalty have always moved the seasonal trends of fashion. The advertising media also contributes equally to update us about the daily style checks.

Fashion in India, a land rich in culture and tradition, has evolved through the centuries. This country, rich in culture represents a kaleidoscope of changing trends and traditions. Here, clothes perform different functions depending on the occasion. Be it festivals, parties, profession, or just a matter of reflecting attitude ... fashion is simply 'in'.

Right from women who sport a dash of vermilion in the parting of their hair, to professionals on the go who wield the ladle and the laptop with equal ease, fashion forms an integral part of their lives. Today, fashion does not necessarily mean glamour, or the urge to follow the current trends. It is more a way of life, a reflection of inner beauty, where the intellect shines through, complete with comfort quotient.

Fashion not only highlights the social history and the needs of person but also the overall cultural aesthetic of the various periods. The evolution of fashion dates back to several hundred years and as our attitude and culture change, fashion comes along with it.

In India, the fashion scenario was different in different political periods. During the British rule in India, the fashion trend within high society was strongly influenced by the British fashion style and western clothes became a status symbol in India.

Again during 1930s, emergence of different ideologies like communism, socialism and fascism imparted a more feminine and conservative touch to the women's fashion. However, the period also witnessed the predominance of body hugging dresses with dark shades. The foundation of the Indian cinema also proved to be the strongest influence on revolutionising the fashion scene in those days.

1940s was a decade marked by the second World War and the ensuing independence of India. Hence, the period portrayed relatively simple yet functional women's clothing. During 1950s, the advent of art colleges and schools led to popularity of narrow waist and balloon skirts with bouncing patterns. Also, the adoption of khadi by Mahatma Gandhi made khadi garments a rage among women.

In the 1960s, the sweeping changes in fashion and lifestyle resulted in highly versatile fashion trends. In 1970s, the traditional materials were exported in bulk to other nations.

Thus, excess of export materials were sold within the country itself, which resulted in popularity of international fashion in India.

During 1980s and 90s, the advent of television and other advertising means gave a new edge to the Indian fashion scene. Influenced by ideas of several foreign designers, new design and pattern were introduced into garments. During these periods, power dressing and corporate look were the style statement. The revival of ethnicity was also witnessed in these decades.

Fashion trends keep changing and most fashion divas and models are the one to make them. The youth is a major follower of fashion trends. Fashion trends also get influenced from Bollywood as well as Hollywood. Metros like Mumbai and Delhi witness the quick changes in fashion especially in college going crowds.

India has a rich and varied textile heritage, where each region of India has its own unique native costume and traditional attire. While traditional clothes are still worn in most of rural India, urban India is changing rapidly, with international fashion trends reflected by the young and glamorous, in the cosmopolitan metros of India. Fashion in India is a vibrant scene, a nascent industry and a colourful and glamorous world where designers and models start new trends every day.

While previously a master weaver was recognised for his skill, today a fashion designer is celebrated for his or her creativity. Young urban Indians can choose from the best of East and West as Indian fashion designers are inspired by both Indian and western styles. This fusion of fashion can be seen on the streets and ramps of the fashionable cities of India.

Fashion in India is also beginning to make its mark on the international scene, as accessories such as bindis (red dots worn on the forehead), mehendi (designs made by applying henna to the palms of the hands and other parts of the body) and bangles, have gained international popularity, after being worn by fashion icons, like the pop singers Madonna and Gwen Stepfani.

In India, fashion has become a growing industry with international events such as the India Fashion Week and annual shows by fashion designers in the major cities of India. The victories of a number of Indian beauty queens in International events such as the Miss World and Miss Universe contests have also made Indian models recognised worldwide. Fashion designers such as Ritu Kumar, Ritu Beri, Rohit Bal, Rina Dhaka, Muzaffar Ali, Satya Paul, Abraham and Thakore, Tarun Tahiliani, JJ Valaya and Manish Malhotra are some of the well-known fashion designers in India.

In India, fashion covers a whole range of clothing from ornate clothes designed for wedding ceremonies to prêt lines, sports wear and casual wear. Traditional Indian techniques of embroidery such as chikhan, crewel and zardosi, and traditional weaves and fabrics have been used by Indian designers to create Indo-western clothing in a fusion of the best of East and West.

Traditional costumes in India vary widely depending on the climate and natural fibres grown in a region. In the cold northern state of Jammu and Kashmir, people wear a thick loose shirt called a phiran to keep them warm. In the tropical warmth of south India, men wear a sarong like garment called the mundu, while women drape 5 metres of cloth around their bodies in the graceful folds of the saree. Sarees are woven in silk, cotton and artificial fibres. Kanjivaram, Mysore, Paithani, Pochampalli, Jamdani, Balucheri, Benarasi, Sambalpuri,

Bandhini are some varieties of beautiful sarees from different regions of India. In the dry regions of Rajasthan and Gujarat men wrap and twist a length of cloth in the form of a dhoti around their lower limbs and a shirt-like kurta above. Colourful turbans complete the picture. In the northeastern regions the tribal communities such as Khasis, Nagas, Mizos, Manipuris and Arunachalis wear colourful woven sarong-like clothing and woven shawls that represent the identity of each tribal group. In urban India the salwar kameez and the churidar kameez, are commonly work by women and the saree is worn on formal occasions. Men wear kurtas and pajamas, or a sherwani for formal wear. Men commonly wear western wear such as shirts and trousers across India. The young and the young at heart wear Jeans, T-shirts, capris, Bermudas and various kinds of casual clothing, which are the trendsetters of fashion in India.

Comparing the past and the present, fashion for people in India has changed over the decades. Not only India, but also the whole world has witnessed changes in fashion statements for both men and women.

Indian Economy

The Indian economy is diverse and embraces a huge area including agriculture, mining, textile industry, manufacturing and a vast area of other services. There is an enormous shift from what the economy used to be in the distant past. Indian economy is the third largest in the world, as measured by 'Purchasing Power Parity' (PPP). Till today, two thirds of the population depends on agriculture directly or indirectly. Indian economy is somewhat socialistic in its approach but presently India is running with other capitalist country.

Pre - Colonial History

Pre - colonial implies to the period before the advent of the British. Indus Valley Civilisation is considered to be the first of the permanent settlements in the urban areas. They usually practiced varieties of traders, which include agriculture, domestication of animals, making sharp weapons from copper, bronze and tin and inter-city trading. Barter system was commonly use in these times although many kings issued coins and revenues were also paid to the rulers. Spices were exported to the Europe, Middle East and south East Asia in exchange of gold and silver.

The rise of the Maratha Empire after the falls of Mughals marked the decline of political stability affecting Indian economy.

Colonial History

Colonial rule brought along with its change in the economic structure of the country. The whole process of taxation was revised, with effect on the farmers, a single currency system with fixed exchanged rates, Standardised weights and measures, free trade was encouraged and a kind of capitalist structure in the economy introduced.

They exported the raw materials and manpower and the finished goods were brought back to India and sold at high rates. These polices were not favourable to Indian Economy. But other developments in transport and communication like introduction of railways, telegraphs and so on were made which affected the economy.

Towards the end of the colonial rule it was seen that development in the Indian Economy was hampered and it was reduced down from its glorious strong economic background.

Post - independence History

There was a basic stress on few things like industrialisation, large public sector, and business regulation, state intervention in labour and financial markets and central planning during this period.

The economy of the country shifted from agricultural, forestry, fishing and textile manufacturing to heavy industries, telecommunications and transformation industries during late 1970s.

In the 1950s the Indian government had undertaken a chain of plans for the economic development. These plans functioned profitably for a while but then again in the long run they showed lese development.

Economic doldrums were a result of structural inadequacies, wars with China in 1962, with Pakistan in 1965 and 71, currency devaluation in 1966, first world oil crisis and few natural calamities.

Contemporary Economy

Major reforms were being made by Rajiv Gandhi in 1980s by restrictions on capacity expansion for incumbents, removal of price control and reduced co-operate taxes. The year 1991 marked the economic liberalisation initiated by the Indian Prime Minister P.V. Narashima Rao and his Finance Minister Manmohan Singh which was in response to a balance-in-payments crises. Other changes, like abolition of the License Raj, direct investments in many sectors, affected economy. More private sector initiatives were taken up during 1980s and 1990s. 1990 onward, India is enjoying constant growth in economy.

At present, India has a modern stock exchange instead of an outdated one. There has been a rise in the growth in many sectors. **State planning and the mixed economy:** Indian economy works on the basis of 5-year plans, which enables an effective and equal distribution of national resources for a balanced economic development. Mixed economy is the merger of the socialist and capitalist economy. India's mixed economy has switched roles embracing capitalist economy to greater extent over the past decade. In India, the public sector covers the railways and postal services. Nationalisation of banks have also taken place, recently phases of privatisation are on the run.

Public Expenditure: Public expenditure in India basically constitutes capital and revenue expenditure. These are included in central plan expenditure, central assistance and non-development expenditure.

Central plan expenditure is for the allocation of resources in development schemes given in the plans of the central government and public sector undertakings. Central assistance is the aids provided for plans of state government and union territories. Revenue expenditure consists of revenue defence expenditure, subsidies etc.

Public Receipts: Tax system has undergone serious changes or reforms over the years. The Union government levies sales tax on intra-state sale of goods, entertainment, alcohol, transfer of property etc. State government's non-tax revenues come from grants, interest receipts, and other economic and social services.

General Budget: The general budget of India is presented by the Finance Minister in the Parliament which is passed by the Lok Sabha. An economic survey is conducted after the budget which involves various NGOs, business people, women organisation and so on.

Rupee: Indian currency 'rupee' is derived from Sanskrit meaning silver and was first introduced by Sher Shah Suri during his reign from 1540 - 1545 CE as history puts it. These days Rupee currency comes in denominations of 1,2,5,10,20,50,100,500 and 1000. Rupee is the only payment of debt accepted in India.

Natural Resources: India has rich reserves of natural resources. Other natural resources in India include mineral resources. Coal, mica, manganese, bauxite, natural gas, petroleum, diamonds etc are the major availabilities of minerals here. India has 4th largest reserve of coal in the world.

Financial Institution: The Reserve Bank of India, National Stock Exchange, Bombay Stock Exchange is located in Mumbai which is the commercial capital of India. India's monitory regulator, authority and supervisor of the financial organisation are the Reserve Bank of India. The RBI issues currency and is also the manager of exchange control. The National Stock Exchange is the world's third largest stock exchange. The stock markets and other securities are regulated by The Securities and Exchange Board of India.

Agriculture: India occupies the second position in the world in terms of farm output. 18.6% of the GDP was contributed by agriculture and related sectors like fishing, forestry and logging and provided employment for 60% of the total workforce. It has increased due to improvements in irrigation, modern agricultural practices, and technological advancements.

Industry: The industrial sector involves the transport, provision of a service such as entertainment, distribution and sale of goods from producer to consumer as may happen in wholesaling and retailing etc. India ranks 14th in the world in factory output, accounting for 27.6% of the GDP and employing 17% of the total working force.

Services: The service industry in India provides employment to 23% of the workforce. It has a massive share in the GDP, amounting to 53.8% in 2005. India takes the 15th position in service output. Information Technology, business process outsourcing etc. fall among the briskly growing sectors, adding up to one third of the total output of services.

Banking and Finance: Banking and finance industry is the strength of Indian Economy. Reserve Bank of India is the supervisor of all major banks in India. Liberalisation has given way for reforms in the banking system. These reforms were made in the nationalised banks as well as in the insurance sectors, private and foreign concerns. All such economic indicators not only measure/analyse the present performance of an economy, but also help in predicting and forecasting India's future growth prospects.

■■■

Discipline

If there is a single element for ensuring success, that element can be summed up in one word: discipline. Discipline, by its very nature, runs opposing to the human nature, which gravitates towards indiscipline and carelessness.

To be disciplined, we must 'drill' into our habits that will cause us to obey thoughts and take actions that will lead us towards our desired objectives. To 'drill' the right habits into our mind, we must bring under control all thoughts and actions that prevent us from moving in the right direction.

But this is easier said than done. Discipline has more to do with 'action' than 'talk'. No amount of positive affirmations or motivational and hidden tapes and seminars will make us disciplined. Anyone can set desired goals and have the motivation to achieve those goals. However, only discipline can 'take' you to your goal. This may mean working consistently for long hours; doing tasks that you would rather not do, but which are essential in the attainment of your goals; foregoing or putting on hold current comforts and pleasures, etc.

None of us is born with inherent discipline. Discipline is acquired through training. We must train ourselves to take the right action at the right time and in the right way. The keyword here is 'training', which implies that discipline is learned. But what makes this 'training' unconventional and more challenging than other conventional forms of training is because it must be drilled at the thought level.

It is in the area of thoughts that behaviours are born, and which in turn lead us to act in one way and not the other. If we can have the right thoughts, then we will behave in the right way and take the right actions. It is the latter aspect of this process that will determine whether we are disciplined or undisciplined; whether we succeed or fail.

Nearly all successful people, especially the self-made super wealthy, can attest to the importance of discipline in the attainment of goals.

They stepped out of the 'comfortable' and 'convenient' and 'trained' their mind to take the right actions. To do this, they chose to 'disobey' the part of their mind that told them to 'take it easy and let it be' and 'obeyed' the part of their mind that insisted that they 'take the right action'. They did not just make decisions; they acted on those decisions.

Acquiring Discipline

To just know definition to be disciplined is not enough; acquiring discipline is also important.

Passion: This is what drives you; what makes you wake up everyday with expectation and hope. Passion propels you forward by enthusing you with a vibrant sense of awareness and conviction. If you can find what drives you, discipline will follow almost effortlessly.

Vision: Disciplined people have a vision of where they want to be at a particular point in time. They never lose sight of where they are going.

Having a clear vision helps you maximise your energy and passion. It enables you to take massive, determined action and bring it to bear on specific goals.

Goals: Discipline is the vehicle that moves you from the point of setting goals to attaining those goals. But goals have to be set first for them to be realised. The fruits of discipline are evident in the number of goals attained.

Consistency: To do the right thing one day and then fail to accomplish the following day's tasks sets you back three steps. To succeed, you must consistently do what must be done until your objective is realised.

Faithful: Discipline requires that you be faithful and trustworthy enough to perform daily tasks comprehensively. Do not pretend that you will succeed when you know very well you have neglected to follow through with the plan. Be faithful; stick to the plan!

Timeliness: You must be disciplined enough to drop whatever it is you are doing and accomplish what must be done, when it needs to be done. Disciplined people do not postpone tasks; for they know that to do so will delay their success.

Eliminate 'noise': 'Noise' here refers to irrelevant tasks, people, places and actions that do not feed into your goal. These are distractions that so often get in the way of your success. Noise is the number one enemy of discipline.

Assertiveness: You eliminate 'noise' by being assertive; that is, by refusing to allow anyone or anything intimidate you to the extent that you fail to do the right thing at the right time.

Learn to say 'no' to anyone or anything that that has the potential to take your eyes off the goal. Also, learn to say no to your own desires if they are not concomitant with your goals.

Tenacity: Discipline requires that you learn to hold on even when calamity strikes. Discipline ensures that you do not give up just because the battle has intensified. Instead, it helps you to be tenacious enough to weather the storm.

Alert: Discipline will demand that you stay alert at all times. Guard your goals with vigour. This is not the time to slumber; you will have enough of that when you attain your goals.

Discipline is 'knowing' what to do and 'doing' it. It is not the 'knowing' that gets you there; it is the 'doing'! Discipline requires an immense sense of control and self-restraint.

The good news is that it can be acquired and inculcated through learning. It may take hard work and patience, but in the end, its rewards are not only fulfilling, but also very enriching.

■■■

Indian Population

Population of a country plays an important role in economic growth. The world has a population of 6 billion. As of March 2001, the total population of India was a little over 1 billion. Despite the fact that India was the first country in the world to have a population policy, not much has been achieved in terms of population control.

India is facing an intense crisis of resources. There is fierce competition for the nation's limited natural resources leading to quarrels between states, between communities and even families. Our land and water resources are being exploited to the hilt. The exploitation of mineral resources is threatening forests, nature reserves, and ecology. Seventy percent of the energy resources need to be imported putting constant pressure on us to export more or face currency devaluation. Over use of resources is contributing to natural disasters occurring more frequently and with greater devastation.

Population is the only non-depleting resource and a parameter of a country's development. In a country like India, where the factors contributing to population growth far outweigh the factors for development, population is no longer a resource but a burden to society. India's population policy has been guided by the perception that a growing population is a serious impediment to development efforts. At the time, census figures showed a Crude Birth Rate (CBR) of over 45/1,000 population — every year; over 45 children were born for every 1,000 people. Many couples have large families as insurance against multiple infant and child deaths. The National

Population Policy 2000 notes that only 44 per cent of India's 168 million couples in the reproductive age group use effective contraception. Reproductive health and basic health infrastructure and services often do not reach the villages.

When India became independent, population growth was seen as a major impediment to the country's socio-economic development and population 'control' was seen as integral to the development process. Population growth was seen as an urgent problem related to economic development with limited resources. At the same time, family planning would benefit both individual families as well as women's health. In 1952, a sub-committee appointed by the Planning Commission asked the government to provide sterilisation facilities and contraceptive advice through existing health services, in order to limit family size, and also institute studies on population. The Reorganised Family Planning Programme ended up focusing on programmes for IUD insertion and sterilisation camps. In 1966, the health minister announced annual targets of 6 million IUCD insertions (20/1,000 population in the urban areas and 10/1,000 in the rural areas) and 1.23 million sterilisations (or 2.5/1,000 population). Sterilisation accounts for more than 75 per cent of total contraception in India, with female sterilisation accounting for almost 95 per cent of all sterilisations. In 1976, the first National Population Policy talked of integrating family planning with general health care, of maternal and child health, the influence of female education, employment and age of marriage on family size, the effect of a high infant mortality rate, and so on. The year 1977 saw the Policy Statement on the Family Welfare Programme. The National Health Policy of 1983 emphasised the need for 'securing the small family norm through voluntary efforts and moving towards the goal of population stabilisation'. In 1991, the Report of the National Development Council Committee on Population proposed the formulation of a National Population Policy with a long-term and holistic view of development, population growth and environmental protection. The Reproductive and Child Health Programme, launched with much fanfare in India in 1997, has generally provided only contraceptive services. NPP 2000's stated goal is to achieve net replacement levels by 2010, by meeting people 'reproductive and child health needs'. Following the announcement of a National Population Policy, a number of states are coming out with their own policies.

The pressing need of the day is to create ideal conditions for acceptance of the need for stabilising the population and how it is an essential element of human welfare and development. The solution to this lies in spreading of education and enlightenment, and in the empowerment of women. Birth control programmes should also be integrated with medical and public health services to make them popular among the masses.

■■■

Unemployment

Unemployment can be described as an economic condition marked by the fact that individuals actively seek jobs but remain unemployed. Unemployment is expressed as a percentage of the total available work force. The level of unemployment varies with economic conditions and other circumstances.

India as a nation is faced with massive problem of unemployment. Unemployment can be defined as a state of worklessness for a man fit and willing to work. The incidence of unemployment is much higher in urban areas than in rural areas. Unemployment rates for women are higher than those for men. The incidence of unemployment among the educated is much higher than the overall unemployment. There is greater unemployment in agricultural sector than in industrial and other major sectors.

Economists and social thinkers have classified unemployment into various types.

Voluntary Unemployment

In this type of unemployment, a person is out of job of his own desire or doesn't work on the approved wages. Either he wants higher wages or doesn't want to work at all. It is, in fact, social problem leading to social disorganisation. Social problems and forces such as a revolution, a class struggle, a financial or economic crisis, a war between nations, mental illness, political corruption mounting unemployment and crime etc. threaten the smooth working of society.

Social values are often regarded as the sustaining forces of society. They contribute to the strength and stability of social order. But due to rapid social change new values come up and some of the old values decline. At the same time, people are not in a position to reject the old completely and accept the new altogether. Here, conflict between the old and the new is the inevitable result which leads to the social disorganisation in imposed situation. In economic terminology this situation is voluntary unemployment.

In Voluntary Unemployment

In this type of situation, the person who is unemployed has no say in the matter. It means that a person is separated from remunerative work and devoid of wages although he is capable of earning his wages and is also anxious to earn them. Types of unemployment in this category are:

Cyclical Unemployment - This is the result of the trade cycle which is a part of the capitalist system. In such a system, there is greater unemployment and when there is depression a large number of people are rendered unemployed. Since such an economic crisis is the result of trade cycle, the unemployment is a part of it.

Sudden Unemployment - When at the place where workers have been employed there is some change, a large number of persons are unemployed. It all happens in the industries, trades and business where people are employed for a job and suddenly when the job has ended they are asked to go.

Unemployment caused by Failure of Industries - In many cases, a business a factory or an industry has to close down. There may be various factors responsible for it there may be dispute amongst the partners, the business may give huge loss or the business may not turn out to be useful and so on.

Unemployment caused by Deterioration in Industry and Business - In various industries, trades or business, sometimes, there is deterioration. This deterioration may be due to various factors.

In efficiency of the employers, keen competitions less profit etc. are some of the factors responsible for deterioration in the industry and the business.

Seasonal Unemployment - Certain industries and traders engage workers for a particular season. When the season has ended the workers are rendered unemployed. Sugar industry is an example of this type of seasonal unemployment.

The problem of unemployment has becoming a colossal. Various problems have caused this problem. There are individual factors like age, vocational unfitness and physical disabilities which restrict the people. External factors include technological and economic factors. There is enormous increase in the population.

Every year India adds to her population afresh. More than this, every year about 5 million people become eligible for securing jobs. Business field is subject to ups and downs of trade cycle and globalisation. Economic depression or sick industries are often close down compelling their employees to become unemployed. Technological advancement contributes to economic development.

But unplanned and uncontrolled growth of technology is causing havoc on job opportunities. The computerisation and automation has led to technological unemployment. Strikes and lockouts have become inseparable aspect of the industrial world today. Due to these, industries often face economic loses and production comes down.

Since workers do not get any salary or wages during the

strike period they suffer from economic hardships. They become permanently or temporarily unemployed.

Today, young people are not ready to take jobs which are considered to be socially degrading or lowly. Our educational system has its own irreparable defects and its contribution to the unemployment is an open truth. Our education does not prepare the minds of young generation to become self-employed, on the contrary it makes them dependent on government vacancies which are hard to come.

Our country, right from the beginning of Five Year Plans, has introduced several employment generating schemes and programmes over the years, but in the absence of proper implementation and monitoring have failed to achieve the required targets.

■■■

Poverty

Poverty is one of the main problems which have attracted attention of sociologists and economists. It indicates a condition in which a person fails to maintain a living standard adequate for his physical and mental efficiency. It is a situation people want to escape. It gives rise to a feeling of a discrepancy between what one has and what one should have. The term poverty is a relative concept. It is very difficult to draw a demarcation line between affluence and poverty.

Even after more than 60 years of Independence, India still has the world's largest number of poor people in a single country. Of its nearly 1 billion inhabitants, an estimated 260.3 million are below the poverty line, of which 193.2 million are in the rural areas and 67.1 million are in urban areas. More than 75% of poor people reside in villages. Poverty level is not uniform across India.

Poverty has many dimensions, changing from place to place and across time. There are two inter-related aspects of poverty-Urban and rural poverty. The main causes of urban poverty are predominantly due to impoverishment of rural peasantry that forces them to move out of villages to seek some subsistence living in the towns and cities. In this process, they even lose the open space or habitat they had in villages albeit without food and other basic amenities. When they come to the cities, they get access to some food though other sanitary facilities including clean water supply still elude them. And they have to stay in the habitats that place them under sub-human conditions.

The causes of rural poverty are manifold, including inadequate and ineffective implementation of anti-poverty programmes. The over dependence on monsoon with non-availability of irrigational facilities often result in crop-failure and low agricultural productivity forcing farmers in the debt-traps. The rural communities tend to spend large percentage of annual earnings on social ceremonies like marriage; feast etc. Our economic development since Independence has been lopsided. There has been increase in unemployment creating poverty like situations for many. Population is growing at an alarming rate. The size of the Indian family is relatively bigger averaging at 4.2.The other causes include dominance of caste system which forces the individual to stick to the traditional and hereditary occupations.

Since the 1970, the Indian government has made poverty reduction a priority in its development planning. Policies have focused on improving the poor standard of living by ensuring food security, promoting self-employment through greater access to assets, increasing wage employment and improving access tc basic social services. Launched in 1965, India's Public Distribution System has helped meet people's basic food needs by providing rations at subsidised prices. Although it has affected less than 20% of the poor's food purchases, the system has been important in sustaining people's consumption of cereals, especially in periods of drought. It has provided women and girls with better access to food and helped overcome the widespread discrimination against female consumption within households. It has also reduced the burden of women, who are responsible for providing food for the household.

The largest credit-based government poverty reduction programme in the world, the Integrated Rural Development Programme provides rural households below the poverty line with credit to purchase income-generating assets. Launched in 1979, the programme has supplied subsidised credit to such groups as small and marginalised farmers, agricultural labourers, rural artisans, the physically handicapped, scheduled castes and scheduled tribes. Within this target population, 40% of the beneficiaries are supposed to be women. Although the programme has reached 51 million families, only 27% of the borrowers have been women. The programme has significantly increased the income of 57% of assisted families.

Rural poverty is largely a result of low productivity and unemployment. The Jawahar Rozgar Yojana, a national public works scheme launched in 1989 with financing from the central and state governments, provides more than 700 million person days of work a year about 1% of total employment for people with few opportunities for employment. The scheme has two components: a programme to provide low-cost housing and one to supply free irrigation wells to poor and marginalised farmers. The public works scheme is self-targeting. Since it offers employment at the statutory minimum wage for unskilled manual labour, only those willing to accept very low wages the poor are likely to enroll in the scheme. By providing regular employment and thereby increasing the bargaining power of all rural workers, the public works scheme has had a significant effect in reducing poverty. It has also contributed to the construction of rural infrastructure (irrigation works, a soil conservation project, drinking water supply). Evaluations show that 82% of available funds have been channeled to community development projects. Targeting was improved in 1996 when the housing and irrigation well components were delinked and focused exclusively on people below the poverty line.

TRYSEM (Training Rural Youth For Self-Employment)

was started to provide technical skills to the rural youth and to help them to get employment in fields such as agriculture, industry, services and business activities. Youth of the poor families belonging to the age-group of 18-35 are entitled to avail the benefits of the scheme. Priority is given to persons belonging to ST/SC and ex-servicemen and about 1/3 seats are reserved for women. Minimum Needs Programme was taken up as an integral part of the 5th Five Year Plan and it was intended to cater to the minimum needs of the people such as rural water supply, rural health, road building, adult education, primary education, rural electrification and improvement of the urban slums etc. With the intention of removing urban unemployment some schemes, such as SEPUP (Self-Employment Programme for the Urban Poor) and SEEUY (Scheme for Self-employment of the Educated Urban Youths) have been launched. These schemes give loans and subsidies for the urban unemployed youths to create or to find for themselves some jobs. The SEPUP had provided financial help for about 1.19 urban unemployed youths in the year 1990-91.

The participation of civil society organisations in poverty reduction efforts, especially those directed to women, has increased social awareness and encouraged governments to provide better services. Cooperatives, such as the Self-Employed Women's Association, provide credit to women at market rates of interest but do not require collateral; they also allow flexibility in the use of loans and the timing of repayments. These civil society organisations have not only contributed to women's material well being; they have also helped empower them socially and politically. Such credit initiatives, by bringing women out of the confines of the household, are changing their status within the family and within village hierarchies. The demands of civil society organisations for better social services have spurred the government to launch campaigns to increase literacy and improve public infrastructure. And, their calls for greater accountability and real devolution of power are increasing the likelihood that expenditures for poverty reduction will reach the needy, especially women.

The Indian state has undoubtedly failed in its responsibilities towards its citizens over the last 60 odd years. There is a need for the state to move out of many areas and the process has been started with economic liberalisation. The process of decentralisation should devote lot more powers, both functional and financial, to panchayats. The lack of transparency and accountability has hampered our economic development at all levels. The problem of poverty persists because of a number of leakages in the system. New laws have to be evolved to ensure more accountability. Bodies like the Planning Commission should be modified into new constitutional bodies that can hold governments accountable for their failure to implement development programmes. A strong system of incentives and disincentives also needs to be introduced. The encouragement of non-governmental organisations and private sector individuals in tackling poverty is imperative, as the state cannot do everything.

■■■

Time Management

Time Management is the control and focus of a person's actions for the purpose of improving efficiency. Time management techniques typically involve setting goals, establishing priorities, budgeting the amount of time allotted to a given activity, and planning and scheduling the steps needed to achieve goals.

Generally, time management refers to the development of processes and tools that increase efficiency and productivity.

When we think of time management, we tend to think of personal time management, loosely defined as managing our time to waste less time on doing the things we have to do so we have more time to do the things that we want to do.

Therefore, time management is often thought of or presented as a set of time management skills; the theory is that once we master the time management skills, we'll be more organised, efficient, and happier.

Personal time management skills include:

- Goal Setting
- Planning
- Prioritising
- Decision-making
- Delegating
- Scheduling

The first step in effective time management is analysing how you currently spend your time and deciding how you want to change how you spend your time.

Unless time is managed properly, nothing worthwhile can be accomplished. Time is a unique resource. It is indispensable, intangible, irreplaceable, irretrievable and therefore invaluable. It is equitably and uniformly distributed. A day of every one consists of 24 hours only, no more and no less. Every piece of work requires time.

Time without energy has not much value; for instance, if one is seriously ill the time duration of illness is practically useless. Time is money. Time is also a measure of effort.

There are two modes of time for every person:

(a) Either you have a very 'busy' mind, effectively employing human resources, like working, thinking, remembering, reading, writing, watching, discussing, listening etc., in short, fully utilising your senses. Here you are very busy and involved.

(b) Or at the other extreme, you have an 'empty' mind – for example, whilst waiting for a bus or train, waiting for a doctor or friend, when you do not get sleep or listening to a boring speech or attending meetings – activities in which you are not interested or mentally involved but perforce have to be physically present.

Time can be divided into three aspects for applying techniques of managing it:

(a) *Biological*: Pertaining to bodily functions.

(b) *Social*: Pertaining to self, family and society.

(c) *Professional*: Pertaining to professional activities/time spent at work.

It is essential to maintain equilibrium between these three aspects. Any imbalance may prove to be detrimental to one's physical and mental health and can adversely affect the individual in the long run.

It is essential, therefore, to allocate one's time in balanced manner to the extent feasible to all these three aspects.

(a) **Biological Time:** Adopt the golden mean of moderation among:

(i) Sleep

(ii) Food

(iii) Ablutions / Calls of nature

(iv) Sex / Recreation

(v) Physical Exercise

It is advantageous to establish regularity for all the above activities.

(b) **Social Time:** It is desirable to give time to yourself, your family and for society and the general guide lines are:

(i) **Self-development/self time:** At least one hour per day should be kept for oneself for thinking, introspection, reading and other hobbies.

(ii) **Family time:** Strong family ties and a happy domestic life are the foundations of success in both personal and professional life. One must spend some time with one's family everyday and to co-ordinate activities of family members.

(iii) **Social time:** In order to live in society, one has to attend various social events, like weddings, religious functions etc., where one is not the master of one's own time. Social obligations may entail a substantial portion of time.

(c) **Professional Time:** In this aspect, if one is working, one does not really have a choice as working hours are generally fixed. The aim here is to optimally utilise the available time for maximum output/productivity and self-satisfaction. It is, therefore, essential to plan one's work and that of the subordinates in an efficient manner and also identify 'Time Wasters' and make efforts to eliminate/reduce them. Examples of Time Wasters are:

(i) Infructuous meetings

(ii) Poor communication

(iii) Unwanted visitors

(iv) Disorganised work

The basic cause of time wastage at work can be classified as follows:

(a) Over-staffing is common cause of wastage of time. Since most of the people do not have clearly defined work for the whole day, they often obstruct each other and create unnecessary problems.

(b) Time is wasted on account of faulty organisation of work. Work is not planned sufficiently in advance.

(c) There is enormous wastage of time and effort due to various meetings often at various locations, which are not properly directed and drag on endlessly.

(d) Time is often wasted because the relevant information is not readily available or the information available is inaccurate. Similarly collection, storage and distribution of unnecessary information is wasteful.

Though one has to evolve one's own technique of time management depending on the circumstances, the three cardinal principles are:

(a) **Span of Attention:** There is a natural limit to how long one can concentrate on a particular activity or task. This is called span of attention.

(b) **Provisions of time in adequate chunks:** If any important work is to be done, time must be made available in sufficiently large chunks. For example – If a job takes 20 minutes, it is of no use to allocate time at the rate of 5 minutes a day for 4 days. Time used in such driblets is utterly wasted. For important work, one requires sufficient time at a stretch.

(c) **Concentration:** Concentration is essential for effective utilisation of time. This as a matter of practice is necessary to avoid all interruptions. It is also necessary to focus attention on one task at a time.

Time Management is essentially a matter of self-discipline, though it is affected by external factors. The aim should be to identify and minimise both internal and external Time Wasters to the extent feasible. One has to cultivate the art of enjoying essential both work and leisure. It is essential to maintain equilibrium between biological, social and professional time for improving one's effectiveness.

■■■

Natural Disasters

A natural disaster is any natural phenomenon which causes such widespread human material or environmental losses that the stricken community cannot recover without external assistance Examples include earthquakes, cyclones, storms, floods, drought, bush/ forest fire, avalanches etc.

The Indian sub-continent is prone to several types of natural disasters. These disasters take a heavy toll on human lives and resources causing economic, environment and social losses. Natural disasters affect the rural community the most, as they are vulnerable to economic changes, and have no alternate means of livings. Natural disasters destroy infrastructure, cause mass migration, reduction in food and fodder supplies and sometimes leads to drastic situations like starvation.

Floods

Floods are a regular feature of Eastern India where the Himalayan rivers flood large parts of its catchments areas, uprooting houses, disrupting livelihoods and damaging infrastructure. The rivers originating in the Himalayas carry a lot of sediment and cause erosion of the banks in the upper reaches and over-topping in the lower segments. The most flood-prone areas are the Brahmaputra and Gangetic basins in the Indo-Gangetic plains.

The other flood-prone areas are the north-west region with the rivers Narmada and Tapti, Central India and the Deccan region with rivers like the Mahanadi, Krishna and Kauveri.

The floods in Bihar in 2008 were one of the worst the

country has seen. Floods in urban areas are rare. Streets do fill up with water, but drainage systems are usually in place to take care of excessive water logging. However, in July 2006, the county's business hub, the city of Mumbai, was rendered completely chaotic for several days as 942mm of rain lashed down. As with most 'natural' disasters, in this one too, man had a role to play. The rapid and constant development of the city and the flouting of rules and regulations caused blockage and choking of the Mithi river that flows through a part of the city and used to carry off excess water to the sea. Violations of coastal regulation zone rules, development on green and no-development zones, building on areas marked for parks and open spaces all of this ensured that what little open space the city now had was not enough to absorb heavy rain. An ancient and badly maintained drainage system added to the problem.

Drought

In 2001, more than eight states suffered the impact of severe drought. Analysis of rainfall behaviour in the past 100 years reveals that the frequency of below-normal rainfall in arid, semi-arid, and sub-humid areas is 54 to 57%, while severe and rare droughts occur once every eight to nine years in arid and semi-arid zones.

The drought of 2002 was officially acknowledged by the India Meteorological Department (IMD) as the 'first-ever all-India drought year', since 1987. The aggregate rainfall received by the country as a whole during the year's monsoon season from June to September 2002, at 735.9 mm, was 19.35 % below the historical long period average (LPA) of 912.5 mm for this period. In July 2002, rainfall deficiency dropped to 51%, surpassing all previous droughts.

The drought impacted 56% of the land mass and

threatened the livelihoods of 300 million people across 18 states.

Cyclones

The states most exposed to cyclone-related hazards, including strong winds, floods and storm surges, are West Bengal, Orissa, Andhra Pradesh and Tamil Nadu along the Bay of Bengal.

The impact of these cyclones is confined to the coastal districts, the maximum destruction being within 100 km from the centre of the cyclone and on either side of the storm track.

The worst devastation takes place when and where the peak surge occurs at the time of the high tide.

Stretches along the Bay of Bengal coastline have the world's shallowest waters, but the relatively dense population and poor economic condition complicate the situation. The population density in some of the coastal districts is as high as 670 persons per square km.

Cyclones have a devastating effect on the economy and lives of the people in the affected districts. A very large population in the affected districts loose its source of livelihood. Public infrastructure suffers extensive damage. The economy of the state suffers a serious setback. This has an adverse impact on the development of the state.

Earthquakes

During the International Decade of Natural Disaster Reduction (IDNDR), India suffered the adverse impact of several earthquakes, the most significant being in Uttarkashi, Latur and Jabalpur. Some of the most devastating earthquakes in India in the past include the Kashmir earthquake in 2005, the Kutch earthquakes 1819 and 2001, the Shillong earthquake of 1897, the Kangra earthquake of 1905, the Bihar-Nepal earthquake of 1934, the North-East and Assam earthquake of 1950, the Anjar earthquake in Gujarat of 1956, etc. The Seismic Zonation Map of India shows the north-eastern states, the Kutch region of Gujarat and Uttarakhand as most vulnerable.

What made the earthquake more tragic was that many parts of the state were reeling under a drought for the second successive year. Kutch was facing drinking water and fodder scarcity. Men had migrated for work leaving women and children behind. Thus it was the poorest and the most vulnerable who were affected.

The peninsular part of India comprises continental crust regions, which are considered stable as they are far from the tectonic activity of the boundaries. Although these regions were considered seismically least active, an earthquake that occurred in Latur in Maharashtra on September 30, 1993, measuring 6.4 on the Richter scale caused substantial loss of life and damage to infrastructure.

Tsunami

One of the most devastating disasters of the 21st century was the Asian tsunami that wreaked havoc in 11 countries on December 26. 2004. A tsunami is a series of ocean waves generated by sudden disturbances in the sea floor, landslides, or volcanic activity. In the ocean, the tsunami wave may only be a few inches high (typically 30-60 cm), but as they race onto shallow water regions their speed diminishes which results in increase in the height of the wave. Typical speeds in the open ocean are of the order of 600 to 800 km/hr. The tsunami's energy flux, which is dependent on both its wave speed and wave height, remains nearly constant. When it finally reaches the coast, a tsunami may appear as a series of massive breaking waves.

Experts warn that as a consequence of climate change, natural disasters like floods from rising sea levels, droughts and heavy rainfall will increase, impacting peoples and economies more dramatically than before. Developing countries that do not have proper preventive and coping strategies in place will suffer the most.

Disaster Management in India

Many international organisations, voluntary agencies and national governments have been working towards reducing the impact of disasters and minimise the loss of life and property on account of man-made and natural disasters. These efforts have been directed at identifying the vulnerability of areas and local communities and developing organisational systems and institutional capacity for risk reduction and disaster response programmes.

In India, the Disaster Management Act, 2005 was enacted on December 26, 2005 to develop plans for prevention and mitigation, and procedures to strengthen capacity building and awareness among people. The Act also permits states to have their own legislation on disaster management.

Under the Act, a ten-member National Disaster Management Authority (NDMA) was constituted with the prime minister as the chairperson. The Authority, with the assistance of the National Executive Committee (NEC) of Secretaries is responsible for:

- Preparing national policies, plans and guidelines for disaster management.
- Approving disaster management plans developed by the states.
- Coordinate enforcement and implementation of the policy and plan.

- Arrange for funds and take effective measures for disaster prevention, mitigation, preparedness and capacity management.
- Provide assistance to countries affected by disasters.

Each state has its own disaster management authority, which is chaired by the chief minister. The state authority, assisted by a State Executive Committee, forms policies and plans for disaster management in the state. A district disaster management authority has also been established by every state in each district. The district authority is headed by the district magistrate.

The local authority trains its officers and employees and maintains the necessary tools and equipments for relief and rescue operations. It also ensures that all construction projects under it conform to the standards and specifications laid down by the state government.

Under the Act, several institutions and funds at the state and district levels were setup.

The Act requires every ministry or department of the Government of India to set aside funds in its annual budget for the activities and programmes set out in its disaster management plan.

Natural disasters result in huge unemployment and under-employment problems. Measures such as building cyclone shelters, a forestation in coastal areas etc have been undertaken to respond to cyclones. Reconstruction projects have been taken up in areas affected by major calamities by designing structural mitigation schemes. The activities consist mainly of housing and public infrastructure, drainage and rural water supply, expansion of road and communication networks, and shelter belt plantations.

Despite these measures, the task is very complex in a country of India's size and diversity. Population pressure, environmental degradation, migration, poverty, illiteracy and unplanned urbanisation are some of the major factors contributing to increased risk and vulnerability. Non-structural disaster mitigation efforts need to be accelerated in the country. It is necessary to emphasise the links between disaster mitigation and development plans, the development of effective communication systems, the application of latest information technology, risk reduction and risk transfer options like insurance, extensive public awareness and education campaigns in vulnerability reduction, legal and legislative support, the involvement of the private sector, the strengthening of the institutional framework for disaster response at the national, state and district levels, the applications of remote sensing, geographical information system, etc. Above all, it is important that civil society initiatives be strengthened and supported to ensure that the existing institutional mechanisms deliver the services they are expected to deliver effectively and efficiently.

■■■

Indian Culture

India is incredibly rich in culture and heritage. Few quotations or statements cannot describe the pedestal that India holds in the world map because of its colourful and unique culture.

From the times of Mauryas, Cholas, Mughals to the period of British Empire, India has always been famous for its traditions and hospitality. The warmth in the relations and euphoria in celebrations make our country stand out distinctively. The country's liveliness and generosity attract a number of tourists. The cuisines, festivals, music, literature, and theatre. Everything is 'special' in this 'land of gods'.

Traditional yet Contemporary

The Indian culture has never been rigid and that's why it's surviving with pride in the modern era. It timely imbibes the qualities of various other cultures and comes out as a contemporary and acceptable tradition. That is what unique about the Indian culture. It moves on with the time. There are certain things about India that are famous worldwide.

Way of Greeting

'Namaste' - for an Indian it's a way common way of greeting outsiders and elders. Both palms placed together and raised below the face not only show the respect for others but it also makes you feel the affection in the greeting. It is for sure that no 'hello' or 'hi' can create that magic.

Flower Garlands

Indian people are also famous for welcoming with flower

garlands. In the Indian marriages, the exchange of garlands between bride and groom is a ritual in itself. People also offer flower garlands to gods and goddesses during their prayers.

Indian Marriages

Time has changed but the lavishness has always been an integral and indispensable part of Indian marriages. In India, marriage is still taken as an institution where not two people but two families get united. So, it always calls for boisterous celebrations full of music and dance. Within India, every caste and community has its own way of performing the rituals of marriage.

Indian Dresses

Beauty of Indian women lies in the clothes she wears. Very traditional and ethnic yet contemporary Indian Saris are famous worldwide. It is worn with a blouse that covers the upper part of the body. In rural parts a version of sari, called ghagara -choli is very much popular. In order to have a graceful and complete look, women folk carry a duppatta, which is a soft and delicate material of reasonable length thrown over the shoulder. Though with slight variations, Salwar kameez is a dress that is famous in every part of India.

For the men, there is no dearth of variety. From dhoti kurta to shirt pants, an Indian man prefers everything that fits well and looks good. But, traditionally you can see north Indians wearing kurta pajama, dhoti kurta or sherwani on formal celebrations whereas south Indian men prefer lungi with shirt.

Indian Jewellery

Unique designs, artistic looks and creativity have always been a part of Indian jewellery. Made up of gold and silver, the jewellery actually represents the culture and tradition of India. In rural

India, a resinous incrustation called lac is used for the personal ornamentation. Specialty of Gujarat and Rajasthan, the lac bangles and bracelets are worn and liked by the women of all states.

Mehandi

Mehandi or henna is a kind of paste that is designed on the palms on the women on special occasions like engagement, marriage or festive celebrations. The paste is applied for few hours or overnight and washed when it gets dried completely. This gives reddish-brown colour to the palms. In certain parts of India, mehandi is a special kind of ancient folk art.

India-Religiously

Hindu, Muslim, Sikh, Christian, Buddhist, Jain or Zoroastrian; one can find people of all religions here in India. India is a secular state and every citizen enjoys an equal right of choosing and following a particular religion.

So many religions and so many pilgrimages, but still people are united. It is just because of the Indian values that bind people together. These values weave people together just like beads in a string.

Worshipping Nature

Indians worship nature and that's what unique about its culture. All the religions here start the day with morning hymns and these rich values are inculcated into the kids since childhood. Morning prayers and moral education are also very important parts of the education system in India.

Here, people are not judged by caste, colour or creed. They are judged by their values and this is what makes India a unique place to live.

Everything is Artistic Here!

Nowhere in the world you can find such a great variety in performing and visual arts that you can find in India. From a roadside show to a highly sophisticated drama in the theatre, you can find anything and everything here.

Indian art can be categorised into two main categories- performing arts and visual arts.

Performing Arts: Dance, drama, theatre or music, every art is unique in itself. Indian classical dances like Bharatnatyam, Kath Kali, Kathak, Manipuri, Odissi and Kuchipudi mainly follow the codes of natya shastra, mythology and classical literature and epics like Ramayana and Mahabharta. Another kind of performing art is theatre.

Though folk theatre prevails in each and every language and region, the professional theatre is popular only in big urban areas or metropolitan cities. Uniqueness of Indian theatre is the puppet show.

Films are another kind of performing arts for which India is quite popular in the world. The country produces more than 1000 movies every year and these movies are not only popular in the domestic market but also have a wide viewership in the Asian and European countries.

Visual Arts: Beauty lies in the eyes of beholder. But, if you look at the sculptures and paintings in India, then you cannot live without saying that the beauty lies in the hands of Indian Artists.

India's history in the paintings is prominently visible in the caves of Ajanta and Ellora, Buddhists palm leaf manuscripts and Jain texts. The creativity and use of colours has always been graceful and unique in the Indian paintings. Keeping their culture and tradition in mind, Indian artists also imbibe the qualities of other European artists and this gives a contemporary look to the Indian paintings with a traditional touch.

A very ancient and aesthetic kind of visual art in India is pottery. In this form of art, lumps of clay are hand-molded to form toys and deities of worship. Terracotta and blue gaze are the two main varieties of pottery that are famous in India.

Celebrations

Celebration is a fundamental part of every Indian's life. From January to December, every month comes with a particular fair or festival. Makar Sakranti, Basanti Panchami, Holi, Ram Navami, Janamashtami, Diwali, Eid, Mahavir Jayanti, Buddha Purnima, Guru Purv and Christmas... festival of every religion has a significance and it is celebrated in a boisterous way.

Here, people don't need a floor to dance. Celebrations on streets during Durga Puja, Ganesh Chathurthi, Janamashtmi and Holi show the real dancing talents of Indians.

Not only this, the country is famous everywhere for the handicrafts melas and fairs that it organises during particular intervals.

It Doesn't Have Just One

Number of religions, number of states... and so number of cuisines. If north India has chole bhature, tanduri chicken, rajma chawal, kadi chawal, dhokla, daal baati churma and biryani to relish, then our south India is not behind in the race. From masala dosa, rava uttpam, rasam, sambar-lemon rice to toran, appam, meen; the south Indian cuisine has a great variety to offer. The concept of Thali is very famous in India. A thali is served in a very traditional form and in this you can enjoy the complete variety available in a particular cuisine.

The variety in Indian masalas like black pepper, coriander seeds, and tamarind, cardamom, saffron and cumin seeds not only enhance the flavor of the food but also add nutritive value to it. The Indian food is incomplete if you don't get something sweet in the end.

Despite so many diversities, people in India are united and they feel proud of their culture and tradition. On the world stage, either through international film festivals or through beauty pageants, India displays regularly its talent and culture. Many rulers came but none could harm its culture; rather Indians preserved the good values of their cultures. The flexibility and movement with time have made Indian Culture fashionable and acceptable too.

■■■

Child Labour

Child Labour, consisting of children below 14 years of age, is defined by the International Labour Organisation (ILO) as type of work performed by children that deprives them of their childhood and their dignity, which hampers their access to education and acquisition of skills and which is performed under conditions harmful to their health and their development. Children are the greatest gift to humanity and the same gift is being misused for personal gains as child labour.

Child labour is harmful to the health of the children, it is a barrier to their education, and it denies them a happy childhood. Child labour is common in agriculture, domestic service, the sex industry, the carpet and textile industries. Employers in these industries buy children from their debtors or through the labour contractors.

Sometimes, children work to help pay off a loan incurred by the family. In some cases the parents give their children to outsiders to work without pay in exchange for better living conditions in wealthy houses.

Child labour has a hostile penalty on the health of the children working in conditions that may endanger their health, such as in stone quarries, tanning leather, and electroplating metals. They work without any protective clothing or equipment. Children in different occupations face different fatal diseases. Children employed in stone cutting, brick factories, granite quarries and slate factories face the risk of silicosis caused from exposure to silica.

Tuberculosis is another disease faced by children in pottery related industries. These children also suffer from malnutrition due to their poor living conditions. Child labourers work for most of the time. In some cases they work for 16 hours a day. This deprives the child time to seek education, which is essential for the overall development and future progress of the child. Some children are bound by their employers as slaves and have to work all the time. In some cases the poverty of the household and low level of parental education are responsible for child labour. The value of education is less important to the parents than the income the child earns for them.

In the present money-oriented environment, the parents consider putting their child to work a better education method than schooling as work assures survival and better future prospects. This is due to the failure of many graduates to get a job, which is evident from the high level of unemployment existing among them. Young boys are put into agriculture and other activities as soon they are old enough to perform the tasks. Girls are made to do household and domestic work as soon as they learn to do them. These children do not get time to play with other children of the same age group. Their friends are children they work with and not whom they play with. They even have little time to seek the love and affection of their parents. On the other hand, these children share the burden of financial responsibility with their parents. Malnutrition is widespread among child labourers. They also receive less or no education compared to their rich counterparts. They are made to do menial and low level jobs that hurt their self-esteem at a very young age. This may hamper their normal development.

Child labour has certain positive aspects also. It is the only means for orphans to earn their living. These unfortunate children who loose their parents at an early age and have no relatives to support them have to depend on working at their small age. In many cases through the practice of child labour the children help and support their parents to settle their financial obligations and to earn money to support the family. People living below poverty line have no other option than to force their children into working in factories and other places for wages. Some parents force their children into the child labour market because they consider it as a part of socialisation process that introduces a child to work activities and teaches survival skills. For households that have low income, any hindrance in the path of income creates complications in the survival of the family, as they do not have enough savings or credit facilities to support them in case of emergencies. This encourages the parents to send their children for work as it helps to face the risk of fall in income or loss of work by any member of the family.

Many organisations and people around the world are engaged in activities to eradicate child labour from the face of the world. For this, they favour policies which worsen the conditions of the victims of child labour instead of improving their living conditions. Such organisations favor the method of taxing heavily the goods that are produced by employers using child labour, to discourage them from employing children. Some organisations persuade people not to buy products of companies that use child labour. The organisations make little effort for providing alternative facilities to the child labourers that may be beneficial to them. Such aggressive methods to eradicate child labour would be properly successful only if they are accompanied by measures and programmes that insure households a regular income. Though child labour supports many poor people, efforts should be made to eliminate it in a manner that does not worsen the condition of the poor people. Programmes should be introduced that provide the unemployed with jobs with adequate salaries. Centers that support the orphans and provide them with free education should be established. Education should be provided to the poor for free and encouraged through different media in an effective manner. Child labour is considered good by many parents of poor families around the world. Therefore, efforts should be made to change the outlook of these parents towards child labour. They should be made to realise that it is in the best interest of their child not to work as working may endanger the health and development of their child.

NGOs have an important role to play in the elimination of child labour. Government does not have the infrastructure to reach every section of the society and particularly the millions who work and live in remote areas. NGOs can act as a bridge between hard-to-reach areas and the government.

In general, all the efforts must be directed towards the elimination of poverty. This way, the world would be a better place for all children when they are brought up in a loving and caring environment and do not have to work and toil right from the early stages of their lives.

■■■

Astrology

Astrology is the study of positions and aspects of celestial bodies in the belief that they have an influence on the course of natural earthly occurrences and human affairs.

Have you ever wondered what the signs of the Zodiac mean? When we turn on the TV, it seems we always see an advertisement on horoscope predictions. People call in and get the predictions they have been looking for. When the newspaper first arrives, some people go to the horoscope section first. They base the entire day or entire week on the report they get. It seems that this phenomenon is something all new, or is it? Astrology has been around since ancient times, even dating back to biblical days.

Astrology has a long line of history and a bright future. The signs of the Zodiac include: Aries, Taurus, Gemini, Cancer, Leo, Virgo, Libra, Scorpio, Sagittarius, Capricorn, Aquarius and Pisces. Astrologers also claim the planets play a role in many key factors. We will also look at astrology as a science; a way to predict and control our life and our destiny. Although many people refer to astrology as just being superstitious others say the predictions are not worth the paper they are written on. Astrology is a phenomenon that dates back to biblical days.

There is an ancient legend, that Adam received the doctrines and mysteries of astrology direct from his Maker and thus by foreknowing that the earth was to be destroyed first by fire and afterwards by water. Astrology has played an important role in our civilisation.

Starting with Adam and even being present in today's society. Different civilisations seemed to be practicing astrology independently. People noticed the Sun in particular had a change on how crops grew. Many people viewed astronomy and astrology as a similar science until the 1500s.

People knew by looking at the sun or what the size of the moon was when to plant crops or even when a baby was going to be born. These early astrologers were searching for their place in life.

A place where they fit into the universe. They believed that every component of the universe was linked together and everyone had their own place.

Every aspect of one's life was based on the planets and the stars. Even behaviour was blamed on the position of the sun!

Astrology is widely practiced today. Even today most farmers have a Farmer's Almanac. This book tells you when to plant your crops, and many people have success. Some won't even think about planting crops without this information. This is a form of astrology, although many people do not realise it.

A popular form of astrology is the Physic Friends Network. This is a 900 number you can call in to see what your sign is and how this affects you.

The astrologers on the Physic Friends Network always seem to know what has happened in the past and what will occur in the future.

Everyone who says they are astrologers obviously are not and it's up to us to use our own judgement to decide.

When you hear people talk about signs of the Zodiac you

often wonder what does that mean? Ancient astronomers noted that the sun makes a yearly journey across the celestial sphere, part of which is represented in the picture by the blue band.

The ancient astronomers associated dates with the constellations in this narrow belt (which is known as the Zodiac), assigning to each constellation of stars the dates when the sun was in the same region of the celestial sphere as the constellation.

Each Zodiac sign belongs to four different elements: Fire, Air, Earth and Water. Fire is a positive element; this element focuses on changing energy from one form to another. Air is also a positive element that is associated with the spiritual part of life.

Earth on the other hand is a negative element that is solid and approves of people on earth. The last element is water this is to a negative element that tends to be mysterious.

Astrologers say they can predict your life through this sign but often you can be very similar to other zodiac signs. Astrologers say that the best way to explain zodiac signs is to 'imagine that your divine spirit is imprisoned in an earthly form, much like animals in a cage.'

They can predict what moods you will be in, what type of person you will marry or even the sports you like to play! These kinds of predictions may or may not come true. Not all astrologers can understand or interpret your true readings. Even if you do not believe in astrology, you can still have a good time. When you pay a minimal charge to find out what the future holds for you, you always want to hear good news. Although sometimes there will be bad news as well.

It is believed that planets tend to affect our lines in many ways. They play an important role in our universe. Research has been done to prove that the weather and earthquakes can be determined through a close look at the planets. The developments are still in the first stages. The future of astrology could be significant in the predictions of dangerous hurricanes and earthquakes. These facts may aid in saving lives. Astrologers served in the king's court in early times to predict many things. When a battle was going to take pace or even the fate of their kingdoms. Many astrologers held influential and well paid positions.

Even today, Astrology is an interesting career for youngsters. Unfortunately, the research is still in the development stages. This research could be beneficial to all of us someday.

■■■

The Solar System

The solar system consists of the Sun; the nine planets, 67 satellites of the planets and a large number of small bodies (comets and asteroids). The inner solar system contains the Sun, Mercury, Venus, Earth and Mars. The planets of the outer solar system are Jupiter, Saturn, Uranus and Neptune. The orbits of the planets are ellipses with the Sun at one focus. Though all, except Mercury and Pluto, are very nearly circular, the orbits of the planets are all more or less in the same plane (called the ecliptic and defined by the plane of the Earth's orbit). The ecliptic is inclined only 7 degrees from the plane of the Sun's equator. Pluto's orbit deviates the most from the plane of the ecliptic with an inclination of 17 degrees.

The Sun is the most important part of our solar system. It is the biggest object and does have about 98% of the whole mass of the solar system. About 1.3 billion earths would fit inside the sun. The sun travels around the galaxy together with planets and other objects bound to it by gravitational forces. The largest of the bodies we call planets, most of which are in turn are orbited by smaller moons or satellites. These objects, together with many lesser masses, are known as the Solar system. The Sun is just a star, one of a hundred billion inhabiting our galaxy alone. Being a star the Sun is an example of the fundamental building blocks of our universe. It formed, 4.5 billion years ago, as the nucleus of a cloud of gas which was collapsing under its own gravitational attraction. At its formation, hydrogen was the most abundant gas, as elsewhere in the universe, and accounted for three quarters of the Sun's original material. This will changes as the hydrogen is burned, and within the very central regions virtually all the hydrogen has been converted to helium. The outer regions have not yet taken part in hydrogen burning. Astronomers have measured the chemical composition of the Sun, and can thus estimate that of the initial solar nebula from which the sun and planets formed. In addition to 78 percent by weight of hydrogen, they find 20 percent to be helium, while only 2 percent remains for other elements such as oxygen, carbon, nitrogen, and iron. Later, as its hydrogen becomes depleted, it will evolve into a giant red star, swelling to engulf the earth and the inner planets. The remnant Sun will fade gradually to oblivion, passing through the white dwarf stage on its way.

Mercury - Mercury is named after the messenger of the Roman gods. It is the smallest of the inner planets and the second smallest in the whole Solar System. It has a very weak magnetic field and - being the closest planet to the Sun - has only a very thin atmosphere of helium captured from the solar wind. The surface of Mercury is very much like the Moon's - with craters, mountains and valleys. Since there is no form of atmosphere, life on Mercury is impossible. Nor will there be any manned flights in the future. However, there will be new unmanned probes sent out, if only to complete the map of the surface. Although Mercury has only a third the diameter of Earth, its density is about the same. This suggests that 65 to 70 percent of Mercury's weight is made up of a heavy material, probably iron. This is concentrated in Mercury's large core. The outer layer is made of silicate rock similar to the Earth's mantle.

Venus - Venus is named after the Roman goddess of love. It is the second planet from the Sun and the brightest object in the sky other than the Sun and the Moon. It was once believed that life could exist in Venus but that has been proved wrong by various probes. In fact, Venus has the most hostile environment in the entire Solar System. The surface temperature is fiercely hot and the atmospheric pressure is crushing. One of the more apparent things that separate Venus from all the other planets in our solar system is that it rotates from east to west (all the other planets rotate from west to east). Because of this, Venus is said to be almost upside down. Conditions may have been better in the past. In the early stages of the Solar System, the Sun was not as bright as it is now and so Venus and the Earth would have formed similarly. When the Sun became brighter, the Earth was far enough away to escape serious damage but Venus was not. The surface temperature rose and the oceans dried up.

Earth - The Earth, the third planet (rock) from the Sun, is the largest of the inner planets and also has the highest density. It is the only planet in the Solar System to be covered largely with water, the only planet with an atmosphere made up chiefly of nitrogen and oxygen and the only body that has a temperature suitable for life of the type that we know. It is also the only inner planet with a large moon - Mercury and Venus have none and the Martian moons are small. If the conditions on the Earth changed even slightly, the life as we know it could die out. The Earth's rotation period is not constant. It is slowly lengthening due to tidal friction between the oceans and the sea floor. This is caused by the influence of the Moon. Our Moon The Moon has fascinated mankind throughout the ages. By simply viewing with the naked eye, one can discern two major types of terrain: relatively bright highlands and darker plains. Current knowledge of the Moon is greater than for any other solar system object except Earth. This lends to a greater understanding of geologic processes and further appreciation of the complexity of terrestrial planets. The relatively bright, heavily cratered highlands are called terrae. The craters and basins in the highlands are formed by meteorite.

Mars - Mars is the fourth planet from the Sun and the seventh largest. It is sometimes referred to as the Red Planet. The name of the month March derives from Mars. Mars has been known since prehistoric times. Except for Earth, Mars has the most highly varied and interesting terrain of any of the terrestrial planets.

One being Olympus Mons, the largest mountain in the Solar System rising 24 km (78,000 ft.) above the surrounding plain. Like Mercury and the Moon, Mars appears to lack active plate tectonics at present; there is no evidence of recent horizontal motion of the surface such as the folded mountains so common on Earth.

Jupiter - Jupiter is named after the king of the Roman gods. It is the largest planet in the Solar System, the fifth planet from the Sun and the first of the outer planets Jupiter has had a dominant effect on a large part of the Solar System. It is likely that Jupiter's huge gravity has prevented a planet from forming in the area now occupied by the Asteroid Belt. Jupiter has a magnetic field 20,000 times stronger than that of the Earth's, having a devastating effect on its moons.

Saturn - Saturn is the sixth planet from the Sun and the second largest: In Roman mythology, Saturn is the god of agriculture and has been known since prehistoric times. Galileo was the first to observe it with a telescope in 1610; he noted its odd appearance but was confused by it.

Early observations of Saturn,were complicated by the fact that the Earth passes through the plane of Saturn's rings every few years as Saturn moves in its orbit Like Jupiter, Saturn is about 75% hydrogen and 25% helium with traces of water, methane, ammonia and rock, similar to the composition of the primordial Solar Nebula from which the solar system was formed.

Uranus - Uranus is the forth largest planet in the Solar System and the seventh from the Sun. Named after the father of Saturn, Uranus is a blue-green colour due to the methane in its atmosphere. Its magnetic axis is at 60 degrees to its axis of rotation. The unusual axial tilt may have been caused by a collision by a large body early in Uranus' life.

Scientists must await a new space mission. Uranus is composed primarily of rock and various ices, with only about 15% hydrogen and a little helium (in contrast to Jupiter and Saturn which are mostly hydrogen).

Neptune - Neptune named after the Roman god of the sea - was discovered using mathematic calculations based on the orbit of Uranus. It is the third largest planet in the Solar System and is usually the second last planet in distance.

Because of Pluto's eccentric orbit, Neptune is the last planet for 20 years every 247 years. Neptune was the last planet until recently, when Pluto past it with its orbit and became the last planet again.

Pluto - Pluto was discovered on February 18, 1930, making it the last planet found in our Solar System. Pluto is usually farther from the Sun then any of the nine planets. Ground-based observations indicate that Pluto's surface is covered with methane ice and that there is a thin atmosphere that might freeze and fall to the surface as the planet moves away from the Sun.

Pluto has one moon – Charon – its surface composition seems to be different from Pluto's. The moon appears to be covered with water-ice rather than methane ice. Its orbit is gravitationally locked with Pluto, so both bodies always keep the same hemisphere facing each other.

On August 24, 2006, the International Astronomical Union (IAU) formally downgraded Pluto from an official planet to a dwarf planet. According to the new rules, a planet meets three criteria: it must orbit the Sun, it must be big enough for gravity to squash it into a round ball, and it must have cleared other things out of the way in its orbital neighborhood. The latter measure knocks out Pluto and 2003UB313 (Eris), which orbit among the icy wrecks of the Kuiper Belt, and Ceres, which is in the asteroid belt.

Asteroids - Asteroids are rocky and metallic objects that orbit the Sun but are too small to be considered planets. They are known as minor planets. Asteroids range in size from Ceres, which has a diameter of about 1000 km, down to the size of pebbles. Sixteen asteroids have a diameter of 240 km or greater.

They have been found inside Earth's orbit to beyond Saturn's orbit. Most, however, are contained within a main belt that exists between the orbits of Mars and Jupiter. Asteroids are material left over from the formation of the solar system. One theory suggests that they are the remains of a planet that was destroyed in a massive collision long ago.

Meteors and Meteorites - The term meteor comes from the Greek 'meteoron', meaning phenomenon in the sky. A meteoroid is matter revolving around the sun or any object in interplanetary space that is too small to be called an asteroid or a comet. A meteorite is a meteoroid that reaches the surface of the Earth without being completely vaporised. Meteorites have proven difficult to classify, but the three broadest groupings are stony, stony iron, and iron. The most common meteorites are chondrites, which are stony meteorites. Radiometric dating of chondrites has placed them at the age of 4.55 billion years, which is the approximate age of the solar system.

Comets - Comets are small, fragile, irregularly shaped bodies composed of a mixture of non-volatile grains and frozen gases. They have highly elliptical orbits that bring them very close to the Sun and swing them deeply into space, often beyond the orbit of Pluto.

Comet structures are diverse and very dynamic, but they all develop a surrounding cloud of diffuse material, called a coma, that usually grows in size and brightness as the comet approaches the Sun. As comets approach the Sun they develop enormous tails of luminous material that extend for millions of kilometers from the head, away from the Sun.

Astronomy usually began with the Greeks. The Greek philosopher Aristotle held that the earth is fixed at the center of the universe while Ptolemy based a mathematical model of the moving planets in our Solar System. Nicolaus Copernicus, in 1543, published his hypothesis that the Sun is the center of the universe but since the teaching of Aristotle had been adopted by the church his view was seen as unbelievable.

Five years after the appearance of the great supernova of 1604, Galileo built his first telescope. He saw the moons of Jupiter, Saturn's rings, the phases of Venus, and the stars in the Milky Way. He published the news the following year in The Starry Messinger. At the age of 23, young Isaac Newton realised that gravitational force accounts for falling bodies on earth as well as the motion of the moon and the planets in orbit. This was a revolutionary step in the history of thought, as it extended the influence of earthly behaviour to the realm of the heavens. One set of laws, discovered and tested on our planet, later governed the entire universe. The first of his many seminal contributions to twentieth century science, relativity recognised the speed of light as the absolute speed limit in the universe and, as such, united the previously separate concepts of space and time into a unified space-time.

Einstein's General Theory of Relativity replaced Newton's model of gravity with one in which the gravitational force is interpreted as the response of bodies to distortions in space-time which matter itself creates. Various improvements have been seen in the study of the Solar system over the past few centuries. They have proved better for the mankind in many ways.

■■■

Teen Social Issues

There are many social problems that teenagers go through. The most recognised problems are teenage drinking and driving, and teen suicide. These two social behaviours teenagers go through are the leading causes of teenage death. Alcohol, the most widely used and abused drug among youth, causes serious and potentially life-threatening problems for this population. Motor vehicle crashes are the leading cause of death for teenagers. Society faces several questions, like why do teens drink, what are the results of teen drinking and driving, and how can society change this pattern. Every year hundreds of teens die. Apart from drinking and driving, teen suicide is the fastest growing killer of youth and if left unaddressed it will affect are future generations. Why do teenagers drink alcohol? Peers play the major role in shaping attitudes about alcohol use. Prior to this time, television and movies played the most influential role. The attitudes of parents toward alcohol correlated strongly with the attitudes of their children.

There are several reasons why teenagers give to drinking alcohol which include recreation, rebellion, relieve depression, fatigue, and boredom. Many of them have personal problems at home that make them turn to alcohol. Other reasons are a loved one passing away, fighting with parents, divorce, and separation of family. The main factor of teenage drinking is influence from their peers. Teenagers in our society are pressured into trying out alcohol for the first time to see how it tastes like. If they give in to their peers, they become part of the group, but if they do not they are not accepted into the group. As a result of teens being under the influence of alcohol, they are not aware that once they get behind the wheel they are risking their lives and the lives of other innocent people on the road. Teenagers think it's cool to drink and drive. They feel nothing will happen to them.

A survey concluded, males having higher rates of daily drinking and binge drinking than females, but these differences are diminishing. In foreign countries, while white students report the highest levels of drinking, the causes that lead them to automobile accidents are driver inexperience, driving late at night, having consumed alcohol, speeding, youthful risk, and driving during emotional stress. Many programmes are being offered to educate teenagers and people on how to prevent alcohol-related accidents.

Education can help teens become aware of the consequences of drinking and driving. Yet effective ways of dealing with teen drinking and driving are formal treatment. Teens can be taken to visit a Rehabilitation center, which is a process of putting the treatment plan into action. It consist of education, Group therapy, life story, individual therapy, peer assessment, recreational therapy, coping skills and relaxation therapy, support group attendance, and spiritually. India is one of six communities across the nation to participate in the Rapid Responses Team Pilot Project, which is designed to study whether a team of experts can work with community members to develop effective ways of reducing underage drinking.

The teams are comprised of one expert from each of the following profession: law enforcement, education, prevention, public policy, and strategic planning. Every year thousands of teens die in the United States, not from cancer or car accidents, but by their own hand; they make the choice that they want to die, and they take their life. Suicide is the fastest growing killer of youth and if left unaddressed, it will help bring about disastrous consequences.

Statistics show that more than 13 of every 1000,000 teenager took their life in 1998 in the US, and that number is rising every year. In fact suicide kills teens 3 to 6 times more than homicide. Although suicide rates over the past 40 years are relatively stable, the incidence of suicide among 15-24 years olds has tripled, while the rate among 15-19 year olds has quadrupled. The numbers of deaths by teen suicide are rising quickly, and it must be stopped. Why is it? Those teenagers are committing suicide? There are many factors which lead teenagers today to take their own life. There is the social environmental factor, which suggests that the greater access to firearms has caused a rise in the death of teens. Teenagers can easily kill themselves with such deadly weapons as guns.

Suicide is genetically influenced. It may be the result of an underlying personality or predisposition to mental illness that is inherited. One other cause is the imitative thinking of our youth. The two major causes of teen suicide are the homophobic sentiments of the people and struggles within the family unit. Struggles and problems within the family are also a big factor of teen suicide. Youngsters who commit suicide are somewhat more likely to come from a broken home than are youngsters of the same ethnic group but about half lived with both biological parents at the time of the death.

The absence of a strong relationship to parent-child friction and a significant excess of poor parent-child communication also lead to teen suicide. What can be done to cripple the rise in teen suicide? According to the National Strategy for Prevention of Suicide of the US, there are three steps in the fight against the problem access, illumination, and methodology. They suggest that access to services and programmes dealing with the issue must be enhanced, the public's awareness be broadened or illuminated, and the scientific approach to the problem be continued. The problem is still not being addressed as it should be. Many teenagers are still dying.

In US, at least, the government has now recognised that teen suicide is a national problem and measures for it are now in the works. Teen suicide is a grave national problem indeed. It has taken the lives of many youth already. In conclusion, society is coming to understand that there is a major social problem with teenagers drinking and driving and teen suicide. In regards to teens drinking and driving, society can change the behaviour of teenagers who drink and drive by using community involvement and educating our youth about dire consequences of drinking and driving. We must look towards igniting and mobilising the passion, energy, imagination, and idealism of our youth to make a real difference. It is our role and responsibility to become involved in our youth because they are our future.

■■■

Social Environment and its Impact

Social environment is influenced by one's power and wealth. This, in turn, determines success or failure in peoples' lives. If one were born with a silver spoon in his mouth, he would easily be able to attend a fancy school no matter how intelligent he is or have any luxury he wants just because of power and wealth. On the flip side, if one were born to a poor family in a bad neighbourhood infested with violence and drugs, he would have a much smaller chance of succeeding in life, more especially, going to an upper-class school. It is hard for many poor to go to college because of such high tuition costs. Scholarships are available; but, even though one shows financial need, one still has to have a high grade point average and test scores.

Even if one has a good mind, trying to study in a gang-ridden neighbourhood with constant gunfire isn't easy. With both parents working two jobs, there isn't any parental guidance. Whereas, the affluent, even if busy or working, have the means to insure that their children are supervised and well taken care of. The rich also have the luxury of affording special tutors to help their children while other children are on their own. For example, there are three students, one from a clean, upper-class community, another from a small, middle-class suburb and the other from a graffiti-ridden slum. All three of these students have exceptional GPA's and scored very well on standardised testing. The student from the upper-class community will have the best chance of succeeding. Tuition will never be a problem and chances are that those parents have some pull because of who they are. The middle-class student won't have a great problem but there is still the fact of paying tuition, which would limit the options quite a bit. One may be smart enough to get grants but the family makes too much money. Also, if he sought admission into a prestigious school and it came down to the student or someone richer, the middle-class student would probably lose out.

Some of the many reasons for this are that the affluent family will most likely have been an alumni to that particular school. If not, they will have better connections and will have a more impressive letter of recommendation written for the student. However, the lower-class student would have a much rougher time. Even with good grades, he might lack the opportunities that others may have. Tuition is definitely a problem and with an overworked guidance counsellor, a problem of a poorer school system, scholarship information might be missing. Most importantly, there would be a decided lack of motivation on the part of the school, family and maybe even the student.

Social environment is not the definitive factor in someone's lifetime accomplishments. It is common knowledge that it is difficult to get out of a bad situation such as growing up without any of the advantages others have, but many have managed. There is a way out, it just takes a strong mind and a strong will to do so. If someone is intelligent enough, they can try to go out and grab the recognition they deserve. Social environment as a determining agent is definitely a human-made force. In a society, the poor are regarded with contempt or completely ignored while the rich are seen as having the authority over everything. The poor are seen as undeserving, therefore, not receiving much of an education, if any. In any society, there are always the strong and the weak; and, in this case, the weak are portrayed as the poor by the rest of society. Some feel that the weak in our society should be eliminated because they are no more than mere pests, irritating the rest of society. In my opinion, there isn't much to be done to change the way society thinks.

As long as the elite control businesses and schools, they will still have the authority over what the public thinks and does. The best thing to have is a positive outlook on all situations and never stop trying. If one never gives up, one can achieve his goal no matter how unreal it may seem at the time. The most important thing is never to let society get in the way. One must not fall prey to society's evils and give up. If there were to be a solution, it would have to be bringing more jobs back into this great country of ours. There is also a lack of good, well-educated teachers. Many of the bad neighbourhoods, where the above-mentioned lower class live, are uneducated because there is a shortage of teachers to give them guidance. If schools were cleaned up and rid of all the violence, then more teachers would be willing to teach there.

All of these goals will be difficult to achieve and will take much time and patience to complete. In not too many years, the generation of tomorrow will be the generation of the present. If everyone is open minded, then perhaps the ideas of the past will change and the poor will be considered human beings. But until then, society remains the same and will be very difficult to change. In conclusion, a very optimistic opinion of the future and the way the poor are treated. It will take concerted effort and cooperation on behalf of everyone.

■■■

Deforestation

Deforestation is defined as the action or process of clearing of forests. The act of deforestation could, in a matter of just a few decades, completely strip the earth of trees. Deforestation not only has a phenomenal effect on the ecological balance of the world, but its economic stability as well. Tropical rainforests are disappearing faster than ever before. Eight thousand years ago, when humans didn't have an astounding affect on the world ecosystem, trees covered two fifths of the land. Since that time, the human race has burnt and chopped down half of the original forestland. According to a survey 'The Food and Agriculture Organisation' (FAO) estimated that in 1980, the rainforests were disappearing at a rate of 114,000 square kilometres each year. More recent studies have shown a sharp increase in that number.

According to a study completed by Friends for Earth, some 142,000 square kilometres of tropical rainforests were destroyed in 1989, and a further 200,000 square kilometres seriously degraded. The Amazon Rain Forest is among the leading places ravaged by deforestation. The first estimates of the damage done in the Amazon were made around 1970, suggesting that little clearing of forest had taken place. According to an article published in '*The Economist*' in April 2000, an official survey listed the damage of 500,000 hectares (1.24 million acres) were deforested between 1990 and 1995.

Deforestation has a number of root causes, from agricultural purposes to increasing population. The most significant amount of deforestation is a direct result of agriculture and the need for food from the rising population.

Most of the forest, that stretched along the Atlantic coast was hacked down to make room for plantations of sugar, coffee and other crops as well as to make room for sprawling cities. Throughout history, as the natives moved through the forest, they began to clear small plots of land for cultivation and living.

Once the land was no longer fertile, the fields were abandoned and the rainforest quickly grew back. Cattle ranching is another one of the highest reasons for deforestation. The ranchers cut and burn vast amounts of land for temporary pasture. After a short amount of time, a year or two at the most, the land is abandoned and another large area of the forest is cleared, repeating the cycle.

Once the soil is too poor for farming or grazing, the ranchers move on. Due to the high price of chemical fertilizers, it is more cost-effective for the ranchers to clear new forest than to recuperate the old pastures. Some people believe that the rising income levels in the developed countries around the world is to be blamed for the increased farming and cattle ranching within the rainforests. The higher the income, the more meat and food is eaten.

After all, the rich do eat more than the poor do. Loggers and miners who are in search of gold, oil and tin are also destroying the tropical rainforests. The environmental effects of deforestation are alarming.

Deforestation increases atmospheric carbon levels; is a factor in species extinction; and also increases the frequency of floods and soil relocation. It has been proven scientifically that the earth is warming up, mostly because of the increase of carbon dioxide gas (CO_2) in the atmosphere. It is now believed that atmospheric CO_2 increases when a forest is burnt. The rate of global warming is estimated to be about one percent per year.

If this rise continues, the world will experience a rise of 5°F by the year 2100, making the world the warmest it has been in approximately 100,000 years. A rise of 7°F would mean the earth would be exposed to temperatures not experienced in over 40 million years.

Trees absorb the carbon dioxide and let off the oxygen that humans need to breathe. In essence, trees are the lungs of the world. Burning them releases all of the carbon dioxide stored within the tree's infrastructure into the air that we breathe.

Scientists have proven that planting new trees for the sake of absorbing the CO_2 would not be effective as preserving the existing older trees. That alone is one of the most important reasons to save the rainforests from further destruction. Along with absorbing the CO_2, the trees also absorb much of the rain, softening its destructive power.

When large areas of land are turned into pasture, the run-off into the rivers increases, and thus increases the likelihood of flooding. The forest also plays a large role in the recycling of water. After the trees absorb the rain, they emit water vapor, which is absorbed into the clouds. The clouds in turn let off the water, in the form of rain and repeats the cycle. The less water absorbed by fewer trees is already influencing the rainfall within the nearby towns, damaging harvests.

Logging of the rainforests can also have disastrous effects on the forests. Logging is the systematic removal of choice trees, as opposed to the clearing of an entire area. The tropical rainforest forms different layers of vegetation, each layer creating a separate habitat for the plants and animals that live there. The trees of the rainforests form a canopy, often as tall as 100-200 feet tall, with thick growth of light-loving trees and plants at top. The under story, as underneath the canopy is commonly called, consists of low-light plants and shrubs that thrive on the damp, dark environment.

When only a few choice trees are removed, the canopy is opened up, drying out the forest floor and increasing the risk of fire. The animals of the rainforest are beginning to be as endangered as the trees.

An estimated 50 percent of the entire world's population of plants and animals live within the confines of the tropical rainforest, although those forests only cover two percent of the globe.

The Tamarin is an example of an endangered rainforest animal. The Golden Lion Tamarin has only 100 animals of that species left, due to the destruction of its habitat– the rainforest. The Cotton-Top Tamarin has an extremely small estimated population, also due to the destruction of the rainforest. Both breeds of monkeys are in captive breeding programs and on reserves. The monkeys are only one example close to extinction. The invertebrate life within the rainforest is only recently began to be studied and already over 40,000 different species have been discovered to live within the same patch of rainforest.

Over 150 different species of butterflies were found in one piece of the forest. Scientists admit that there are thousands of species of plants and animals that have yet to be discovered, how do we know for sure that hundreds of un-known species of plants haven't been killed completely off by the inhumane and selfish actions of the human race?

Economically, the effects of deforestation are astounding.

The price of wood has undoubtedly gone up, since that resource is almost wiped out. It is extremely hard (and expensive) to find anything made of solid wood today. The future generations had better become accustom to furniture and homes made of plastics and veneers, since that is what will be left by the time the current generation has used up the available resources.

Most household items, in some way, are derived from the rainforest. Over 7,000 medicines have been derived from the rainforests, and with only one percent of the plants of the rainforest documented, who's to say that there isn't a cure for cancer or AIDS in there somewhere?

We may never know at the current rate of destruction. Many people living within the immediate area of the rainforests have lost homes due to uncontrollable fires, almost all of them directly related to illegal logging.

There have been complete villages that have been swept away in torrential downpours and flooding, attributed to the lack of trees and roots absorbing water. There have even been documented cases where villages were erased in landslides, due to a lack of root systems to keep the soil intact.

On the flip side, some areas are now in drought due to the interruption in the hydrological cycle and lack of rainfall. The lack of water has a direct result on the crop yield, sometimes completely killing the crop and leading to starvation.

Can you imagine all of this destruction and economic hardship because of deforestation? If these effects were more widely known twenty years ago, the rainforests might not be in as much danger. Forests have provided essential resources throughout history.

Currently, they provide the industrial world with numerous

raw materials such as gums, nuts, fruits, wood pulp and timber, and probably most important of all- medicinal plants. Knowing that over a quarter of the world's pharmaceutical medicines are derived from the rainforest, mankind could very well be placing the yet-to-be-discovered cure for cancer on the extinction list too. Half of the world's rainforests have already been destroyed.

Rainforests conserve water, prevent drought and flooding and regulate local climates. When they are cut and burnt, a significant amount of CO_2 is added to the atmosphere, contributing to the global warming, essentially the greenhouse effect. The biological diversity of these forests is amazing- and with all of this, they are still being destroyed. Every person of earth should do his or her part to save earth.

■■■

Creation *Vs.* Evolution

The majority of people in this world believe that a spiritual being created earth. In fact, most religions and cultures believe the universe was created by a 'creative hand,' either a sky god or some other physical object. Think of it, as a trial to see which will win, creation or evolution. It has been the most argued debate in all of history, but creationism is more logical than evolution. To first understand what creation is about, we have to know what creation is. The Bible defines creation as the action by God that brought the universe and all its contents into being. The Bible also states, God created great whales and every living creature that moveth, and so God created man in his own image, in the image of God created he him; male and female created he them.

There are nine articles of evidence pointing weaknesses in evolution, or strong points in creation. The first evidence is that there are no links between the fossil record and present times; therefore, there is nothing to show that evolution actually happened. Second, that natural selection cannot advance an organism to a higher order. The third being that although evolutionists believe life just came about, matter resulted from nothing, and humans evolved from animals, all of these are against scientific and natural understandings. Fourth, even though evolutionists present them as if they were, the hominids' bones and skull records, for example the famous Lucy, the finds are unrevealing and inconsistent. The fifth and sixth articles of evidence are the nine out of 12 hominids that evolutionists use are really extinct apes, and the other three are modern human beings and not part ape. This would conclude that all of the twelve 'hominids' are something other than hominids and are not half-human, half-ape. Evidence seven and eight show that natural selection has practical, social, and logical inconsistencies. The last evidence says that the rock strata finds are better explained by a universal flood than by evolution, which would show yet more proof in the Bible.

The definition of evolution is the complex process by which living organisms originated on earth and have been diversified and modified through sustained changes in form and function. Researcher and British scholar Thomas Robert Malthus first stated that the human population was growing too fast for the food supply. Darwin applied this to animals and plants and came up with the theory of evolution by natural selection. His theory stated that the children of a species intensely compete for survival. Those young that survive to produce the next generation tend to be embodying favorable natural variations and these variations are passed on by heredity.

Therefore, each generation will improve adaptively over the preceding generations, and this gradual and continuous process is the source of the evolution of the species. The notion that populations of organisms can be transformed over generations into descendant population of different kinds has been suggested repeatedly since the early-recorded history of ideas, but if you trace all the species back to their origin, you would get one object. Now, the real part of this argument is right here. How did that one object come into being? It couldn't have happened by mere chance. It did not always exist so there had to be nothing before it. If there was nothing before it, how was it created? Now some would like to say that it was created by the Big Bang, but if we look at the Big Bang theory, it is suggesting that the one object did not just appear that it was created by the Big Bang. This is a contradiction because the Big Bang is supposed to have just 'happened'. The other contradiction to this statement is that by the laws of science matter has to come from other matter, but the Big Bang theory used by scientists states that the first matter just happened at the Big Bang and came from nothing.

Now that we have the facts, we should be able to look at it from an atheistic point of view, and be able to easily crush the argument that the earth might have just happened and evolved into present day. This argument without a doubt shows proof of a Creator. There had to be a Creator because even by the scientific or atheistic point of view, it is not possible for something to come from nothing. So that something, that existence came from God, the Creator.

■■■

Customer-Relationship-Marketing

Marketing and business development professionals are confronting a rapidly different and changing business landscape. The traditional business model that was once the standard is now being transformed due to technology drivers that make advanced marketing and sales capabilities possible. The business model of yesterday supported mass marketing, mass production, and standardised cookie-cutter products and services.

Enterprises will have fall behind the competition if they continue to rely and operate on this substandard model. Today, companies are re-engineering their operations and investing in enhanced IT infrastructures, which enable them to provide customised, personalised, information-rich products and services. The new objective for marketers and business developers involves understanding the needs of their clients and the markets that they serve. This new focus on providing customer value is redefining business processes. Professionals, who understand and anticipate this shift, are positioning themselves ahead of the competition.

There is no denying the effect that technology has had on the way we conduct business. In recent years, technology has begun to play a significantly larger role in all aspects of business, including sales and marketing. Business processes must be re-engineered to incorporate a pro-active strategy for using information and IT to build a competitive advantage over other organisations.

In many instances, the functionality provided by sales and

marketing technology only automates current processes. Therefore, it is imperative that processes are clearly defined and well proven. Automating a poorly understood or followed process usually results in failure. Technology must be used as an enabler to support an already sound sales and marketing strategy.

Beyond automating sales and marketing capabilities, technology is now designed to provide professionals with a wealth of information about their company's clients and the markets that they serve. Companies are now able to collect data about their customers that when analysed and utilised properly, can result in a competitive advantage. Online shopping is a prime example. If a customer makes a purchase, then the transaction is completed and revenue is generated.

However, if a sales transaction is not made, the company still collects the shopper's behavioural data and stores it in a marketing database. The company then has the opportunity to segment and analyze this data in order to learn more about that particular customer shopping habits. An analysis can then be performed to determine why this person did not make a purchase as well as what can be done differently to persuade this person to buy their product. The company can now position the four Ps of marketing: product, price, promotion, and place to better serve it customer.

Due to this process, the company ultimately succeeds in developing a relationship with the customer. The company now knows more about what the customers preferences are and how to offer them. Consequently, the customer has a vested interest in the relationship as well, and is more likely to conduct business with that company in the future.

Though many of today's marketing practices have evolved

due to increasing technology, the marketing environment still centers around the four Ps of marketing described above. However, in order to remain competitive, companies must create a unique set of those four Ps which appeal to each individual customer and sets them apart from their competitors. Target marketing is no longer an efficient use of marketing efforts because a great deal of resources can be lost to uninterested individuals while in the process of trying to capture potential customers.

Because of the potential loss of resources, there is now a movement away from targeting markets to specific individual customers. What is now required is customer-oriented relationship marketing. Many studies have shown that it can cost anywhere from four to ten times as much to acquire a new profitable customer as it does to maintain repeat buyers.

These statistics are one of the driving forces behind the move to relationship marketing, which focuses its emphasis on customer retention rather than attraction. This type of strategy calls for a different type of marketing technique that is customer and information driven as opposed to product driven.

With this in mind, marketers and business developers are now seeking new ways to obtain, manage, and analyze information on their customers. As we are increasingly finding, one of the most effective ways of capturing and utilising customer data for marketing and sales efforts is by investing in technologies such as a Customer Relationship Management Systems (CRMs).

The term CRM describes methodologies, software, and usually Internet capabilities that help an enterprise manage customer relationships in an organised way. From a technological standpoint, CRM can be categorised as the largest compilation of IT concepts to date. It involves moving the ownership of customers away from individual departments to the enterprise level. In addition, its focus is also on best serving the needs of each customer on a personal level rather than serving the needs of target markets as a whole.

The primary functionalities of CRMs are still debated by experts, and often times it varies depending on the purpose the system is intended to serve in that instance. However, the high-level buckets of CRM capabilities can be categorised according to customer service, marketing, and sales.

Although customer service is an important aspect of customer relationship management, it is primarily employed by companies who sell products as well as have call centers and websites to market and/or sell their merchandise. For example, most consulting firms are in the business of marketing and selling professional services. which results in their consultants and client managers having closer relationships with customers.

One of the key reasons that companies invest in CRMs is because they can provide an analysis of customer data that can result in an improvement in process or product. CRMs can achieve an improvement in marketing processes because they help enterprises identify and target their best customers.

CRMs can perform customer segmentation, which helps marketers focus their efforts on where they will make the greatest impact. Before technology-enabled marketing, individuals were usually segmented into groups with others who shared similar demographics or social characteristics. Today, CRMs are able to segment individual clients, perform statistical modeling, and provide profitability calculations in order to detect the relative value of that client to the business.

For companies such as professional services firms, one customer can mean substantial revenue opportunities.

Discovering these opportunities is one of the goals of effective marketing departments. CRMs can aid in this process by providing lead management and opportunity tracking. Lead management technology analyzes company or proprietary data to determine where an enterprise's greatest opportunities lie. In addition, consulting firms can employ the technology of CRMs to track requests for proposals. The technology behind CRMs has the capability of keeping track of which RFPs were followed.

In addition, an analysis can be conducted on those industries or markets from which the company is receiving RFPs in order to determine those areas that are most profitable and therefore focus on in the future. Not only can CRMs assist in identifying opportunities, they can also track marketing efforts against wins in order to determine how effectively a company's campaigns are. Many companies blindly market to current and potential customers without really knowing if their efforts are working. An integrated CRM has the functionality to calculate the percentage of those who responded to a marketing campaign compared to those who were targeted in the campaign. This is an invaluable tool in identifying the most appropriate methods and tactics for reaching current and potential clients. A technique that has long been employed by marketers to get a better sense of their customer's needs and preferences is through surveys and questionnaires. Many CRMs come equipped with tools that can automate and improve upon this process. Survey tools can be used to distribute, compile, manage, and most importantly analyze survey findings. Technologies as common as MS Access and e-mail are capable of distributing, compiling, and managing these findings. But it takes the more advanced functionality found in technologies such as CRMs in order to conduct an in-depth analysis of the survey results. This type of analysis is what makes the survey results meaningful to marketers and business developers. Sales Capabilities of CRMs Sales and marketing efforts often go hand in hand in ensuring revenue and growth within an enterprise.

Hence, much of the information and process improvements, which benefit marketing, can also be used to improve sales efforts as well. Because these two functions are so closely related, its only logical that the technology that enables them is integrated. CRMs provide information, resources, and tools that allow marketing teams to win clients and enable sales teams to generate additional business.

These two departments need to form a partnership in order to ensure their efforts are being focused on using CRM tools to optimize sales and marketing efforts. The backbone of CRM sales automation is a centralised customer database that lets customer information collected throughout the enterprise available to the company's sales force. This provides the sales team with more information to use for prospecting and customer contact. CRMs allow sales people in the field better manage their contacts by creating client profiles as well as records of their historical interactions with the company. Effective and accurate contact management is a vital tool to any client manager.

Client managers need to track who their contacts are in a particular company, what their job role is, where they are located, etc. This information ensures that they are communicating with the right people in the company and keeping key people informed of developments. Client profiles are another essential feature of a CRM. Client managers need the most relevant, accurate and complete data on their clients as possible. A CRM can help make this possible. A truly integrated CRM is an ideal system for collecting and managing customer data. This means that all interactions with the customer are stored in a centralised database for easy retrieval. To a client manager, this information is invaluable. A CRM can create a customer profile based on data received from web registrations, surveys, as well as historical interactions. Information from client transactions can be used to determine customer preferences, needs, as well as activities or events the client has attended. This information can be used when making decisions on how to best optimize sales with that client in the future.

As mentioned previously, marketing and sales departments are increasingly relying on relationship marketing as a means to more effectively acquire and retain clients. In short, in order to stay competitive, companies must operate based on a customer-centric business model. CRMs are at the forefront of emerging sales and marketing technologies, but there are many tools that contribute to this technology's vast functionality.

■■■

Capitalism *Vs.* Socialism

Capitalism and socialism have existed in different societies throughout the world that have been successful at times, but also not so fortunate in its' success at other times in history.

The definition for capitalism would be a form of social system that separates the economy from the state. Capitalism is based upon private ownership of property and every person has the right to live his life in any manner he chooses, as long as he does not violate the rights of others. Individuals are allowed to run their own businesses in a free market in such way that he or she creates the wealth for him or herself. It usually depends on how self-motivated a person is to be self determine how wealth they will become.

If a person is always working hard to make money, they most likely will, compared to a 'bum' who can not get welfare in this type of system.

Capitalists believe that the only purpose of a government is to protect its citizens from force or fraud. They claim that the force is the protection of individual's rights. This is achieved in such ways as the use of police force to protect the rights of citizens at home, a military to protect citizens from foreign attack, and a court system to enforce contracts and settle disputes between residents.

Capitalists also feel that initiating force can only violate rights, thus the government only uses force in relation of those who initiate it. For instance, if an individual can not start his own electric company, it is a violation of his freedoms.

A capitalist's argument towards this statement would be that the governments' legal monopoly on utility companies prevents people from starting their own electric company.

In a capitalist society, all people can start any kind of business they want. The protection or threat of monopoly is not there. If a person wants to take the chance on their own company, even if it is next to one that is successful, the peril is in their 'own hands'. The only law capitalists clearly state, and one must follow is that members of society can not infringe on the rights of others. They give credence to holding individual rights as absolutes, and freedoms as absolutes. From a purely economic view, a capitalist is a person who buys in order to sell for profit.

Socialism is quite different compared to capitalism, almost like an exact opposite. Instead of the ownership of private property, the government plays a large role where society owns social property, such as banks and factories; although they own it through the government.

Socialism is a society where the resources of the society, controlled by workers, are used for the benefit of the whole economy, not just the rich. The government does have control over production and economic activity, but the workers themselves decide what to produce, where to produce it, how much to produce, and how to distribute the product fairly for the benefit of everyone. Philosopher Karl Marx and his followers were convinced that sooner or later alternatives to capitalism would emerge because, "it is already in the process of developing within a capitalist society and we must find a way to overcome the resistance of capitalists and their supporters to achieve socialism." The best definition for socialism is the equal distribution of society's goods to be achieved by the government. It focuses on positive freedoms such as everyone is entitled to the basic necessities: food, clothing, shelter, and a job. This is where the government steps in to help those who are needy and have rational reasons to why the government needs to give assistance to these people by providing programs such as welfare.

The best point that can be said about the socialist system is that there are incentives to good workers, which makes them work harder to get these bonuses. The bonuses can be anything from cash, extra vacation, company parties, and prizes. The working class has the basic knowledge and principles they need to run the economy. Training is given where it is needed, and educational institutions have been refined so we have professionals in the fields where it is more important that the person has extensive knowledge in the subject. For those who are working in a socialist economy the government has made laws all companies must follow, they are also working class principles. All workers should be treated fairly and equally and this is what these laws were made to do, protect the working class. Minimum wage is set so all workers receive at least this amount of pay, and then wages must go up according to their type of job. Also, good working conditions must be provided for safety reasons, no child labour, and no discrimination at the work place are a few laws that have been made.

Capitalists and socialist disagree about certain ideas each group has and criticizes each other's ideas. First, we will start with what capitalists think socialism is. They feel that man must sacrifice his own notions for the sake of the greater good in their economy. They feel that they must also sacrifice their individual mind, which denies them the sole means of survival for man and his nature as a rational being. Capitalists do not regard this system as an ideal. A capitalist's ideal accommodates one standard of life, man's life. The measure of a socialist system consists of the appraisal of, the relationships between men, and institutions that govern the forms of association. In defence to this, socialists say that the workers in a capitalist economy struggle against corporate greed. Working people should work together socially to produce all things together. Capitalists are different and take the wealth that they create to build more capital for himself. They feel as if there is a contradiction between social production and individual capitalist ownership. One capitalist deprives another capitalist of property and more wealth is concentrated towards a smaller and smaller number of people. In order to compete in this type of market things must be cut; jobs, wages, and benefits.

Although, capitalists say that contrary to this highly held belief it is not a system that exploits a large portion of society for the sake of a small number of wealth businessmen. They say that socialism causes the exploitation of labour. They do this by placing monopolies on labour and production and exist merely to follow what a 'spokesman' of socialism has in mind. There are good points and bad points concerning both types of systems, although many feel that socialism has more good points than a capitalist economy, which makes it more successful.

Unregulated capitalism leads to worker exploitation because there is no government intervention to protect workers. Racism in the workplace takes place because there is not a minimum wage set and impedes poorer minorities from reaching economic advancement. They will not have enough money to pay for the high priced items the companies they work for produce. If a minority worker were able to do the same work for a lower wage then it would be in the economic self-interest of the employer to hire that person. The driving force under capitalism is driven by a profit motive because firms want to maximise their profits at all times. The protection against discrimination is not there, but it is provided by a socialist economy. A capitalist's argument against this would be that workers are free to choose who they work for and if they decide that they are going to work for someone who pays less than minimum wage, that is their own fault and should seek work elsewhere. Poor working conditions are also a problem that comes up. With an unregulated economy, immoral businessmen will try to increase their own profits by selling cheap, unhealthy, and unsafe products to an ignorant community. The workers who make the products have unsafe machinery, an unsanitary workplace, and no insurance so if they were to get hurt they would not be safeguarded.

In a free market, the only type of monopoly that can exist is a 'non-coercive monopoly' or one that is earned, in the words of a capitalist. The goal of a welfare system is to help certain citizens when they need financial aid in order for them to be productive members in society. Capitalists do not provide this service and say it is the government stealing money from its citizens on the basis of those with more wealth who have a duty to serve those with less. It may do this, but in the long run it creates a class of fewer people who are dependants and have been given a way restart their lives or begins one. Financial aid for college students through grants and other scholarships is another example of this. The money is going to a good cause to better young adult's education and we can have more qualified workers in various occupations.

Public property belongs to everyone, no one person takes care of it and property with no real owner is easy to pollute. If all property is privately owned, then no one can dump garbage in a river because it will drift into another person's private property, thus violating his or her rights. Capitalists do not have a government, but they do believe in courts, or a way to settle disputes over contracts such as property rights. Also, if the beaches and parks are owned privately and the owner charges money for people to use his land, then it would be in his own self interest to keep it clean so more people will come to his park instead of a competitors'.

Socialism is the better of the two systems in several ways, and more successful. It is the governmental laws and regulations that make them this way. It does not make the economy more complicated or unfair by any means. Socialism is a society where all people who want to work not only can work, but work for a good living, have a say over the conditions of their work, wages, and even who runs their workplace. There are no bad jobs, only low wages and bad working conditions, but under socialism all workers are required to be treated with respect and have a job that gives them dignity. Laws have been made to protect the worker from low wages, poor working conditions, and other types of exploitation. Discrimination against any worker, whether it is because of sex, race, colour, or religion is also illegal. Employers must hire for skills in a person and can not use the excuse such as they do not want a woman working there as an excuse when she is the most qualified. A minimum wage has been set and raises with the economic times when prices also raise. In a capitalist society those who are not given this raise can not make a good living, where as socialists believe that everyone is entitled to this. If a person is skillful then they are paid according to that. Education plays an important role also to help employees reach these skills. Socialism is a society where workers will be trained how to run a society and learn the skills to make good economic plans. Social ownership is not enough. It also means that working people run, operate, control, manage, and own all of this property. It makes decisions as to where it wants to be in five years that affects us for the fifty years, and what plans we are going to make to get there. When comparing and contrasting socialism with capitalism, one can find good in both ideas of systems; it just depends on a person's opinion. Socialism would be the system a moralist would more likely follow than capitalism. It appears that capitalists are greedier and care about what is better for himself or herself than everybody as a whole, whereas highly moral people tend to help others and careless about being wealthy and more how they are treated, along with their fellow workers. They like the government because they feel that the government does provide good programmes for those in need. The key to economic success lies in the socialists' economy because they not only offer freedom for everybody, but a way so all businesses are fair with each other, not only in competition, but also to their customers and employees.

■■■

Importance of Physical Education

As the saying goes – Those who do not find time for exercise will have to find time for illness...

In most of the schools, physical education is part of the curriculum. Apart from maintaining physical fitness, it includes training in the development and care of the human body. It helps a person sharpen overall cognitive abilities and motor skills through athletics, exercise and various other physical activities. Seeing its benefits for the body and its effect on life, the importance of physical education can't be ignored.

Physical education inculcates in children the importance of maintaining a healthy body and teaches then the importance of regular fitness activity in daily routine, which in turn keeps them happy and energized. This helps the children to maintain their fitness, develop their muscular strength and increase their stamina.

Research has proved that children who actively participate in sports, be it team sports or dual and individual sports, have high self-confidence, which is very important for the development of a person's character. Physical education instills the desire to participate, enjoy victory and take defeat positively, developing the overall personality of the character.

By making children participate in sports, especially team sports, physical education also imbibes in them a sense of team spirit. Children learn how to work as a team member, organize themselves and function together towards attaining a goal. This in turn improves a child's overall communications skills and the ability to get along with different kind of people.

Physical education helps one gain knowledge about the overall aspects of physical health. In today's world, several health problems like obesity, anemia, bulimia, and even diabetes, are rampant amongst teenagers. Through physical education, teachers can promote the benefits of healthy and nutritious food and discourage them for having junk food by highlighting their ill effects. They can easily promote sound eating practices and guidelines for nutrition.

Physical education also teaches about the importance of personal hygiene and importance of cleanliness. They guide the students by informing them about the important hygiene practices for maintain health and well being throughout the life. In addition to this, the physical education classes also cover an important aspect that the children have to deal with at the age of puberty.

Apart from health and knowledge benefits that students get from physical education, they also learn how to unwind and relieve themselves of stress and anxiety. Sports and other physical fitness activities offered in the physical education classes are a welcome break for the students.

It won't be wrong to say that children, who learn the importance of health and hygiene in their early ages, tend to grow up to be responsible and healthy adults who are well aware of the benefits of a healthy lifestyle. Children who are provided good physical education are more likely to become responsible adults who know the importance of a healthy lifestyle.

■■■

17. General English for Competitive Examinations

18. Spoken English

19. School Essays, Letters & Phrases

20. How to write & Speak Better English

21. Quote Unquote (A Handbook of Quotations)

22. Improve Your Vocabulary

23. Common Errors in English

24. The Art of Effective Letter Writing

25. Synonyms & Antonyms

26. Idioms

27. Business Letters

Lotus PRESS